DATE DUE   MAR 0 5

JUN 2 8 '05		
AUG 1 0 200		
MAY 2 3 200		
SEP 2 7 '06		
NOV 2 1 2008		
GAYLORD		PRINTED IN U.S.A.

LOVE IT
OR
LOSE IT

Living Clutter-Free Forever

By
Barbara Hemphill and Maggie Bedrosian

Published by
BCI Press
4509 Great Oak Rd
Rockville, MD 20853-1948
www.LoveItOrLoseIt.com

in association with Bedrosian Communications, Inc.
www.MaggieBedrosian.com, and
Hemphill Productivity Institute
www.ProductiveEnvironment.com
800-427-0237

Bedrosian, Margaret McAuliffe & Hemphill, Barbara

Publisher's Cataloging-in-Publication
Hemphill, Barbara.
    Love it or lose it : living clutter-free forever / by
Barbara Hemphill and Maggie Bedrosian. -- 1st ed.
    p. cm.   Includes Index.
    LCCN: 2002111574
    ISBN: 1884798276
1. Home economics. 2. Orderliness. 3. Conduct of life. I. Bedrosian,
Margaret McAuliffe, 1942- II. Title.
TX147.H46 2003   640
                                  QBI02-200648

ISBN # 1-884798-27-6
Library of Congress Catalog Number 2002111574
© 2003 by Maggie Bedrosian and Barbara Hemphill

Cover Design - Anita Brienza, Calibrate Communications
Marketing Consultant - Greg Godek, Bestseller Management

Printed in the United States of America by Central Plains Book Manufacturing
        10   9   8   7   6   5   4   3   2

Federally-registered trademarks property of Hemphill Productivity Institute:
        Clutter is Postponed Decisions®
        Taming the Paper Tiger®
        Love It or Lose It™
        The 24-Hour Miracle™
        The Productivity QuickStart™
        The Art of Wastebasketry™
        The Clutter Trap™

ACKNOWLEDGMENTS

Thanks first to the brave family, friends, and clients who have encouraged us to share their stories. Including families Taylor, Frost, Hemphill, Bedrosian, Atanosian, McAuliffe, Cavarocchi, Carpenter, Orlando, Mullins, Villareal, Larramendy, Gollen, Buonocore, Butler, Lolandi, Mennitt, Willoth, Wester, Barnes, Ogilvey, Maier, Hess, and Paper Tiger Authorized Consultants. They have added the human touch.

Thanks to our publishing support team Greg Godek, Anita Brienza, Kevin O'Sullivan, Art Gliner, Kristin White, Stan Craig, DJ Watson, Florence Feldman, Glenna Salsbury, Leslie Charles, Pam Lontos and the PR/PR team, and the Awesome Authors Group, Mariah Burton Nelson, Lynne Waymon, Sam Horn, and Barbara Feinman. They have added the professional touch.

Thanks to our husbands-extraordinaire, Alfred Taylor and Marty Bedrosian. They have added the loving touch.

DEDICATION

To Cassyn Myers Taylor and Sarah-Anne Bedrosian
The newest lights in our lives

Dear Reader,

Every item around you represents a choice you made. You either went out and selected it, or it came to you, and you accepted it.

Look at that item now with fresh eyes. If you do not know that item to be useful, believe it to be beautiful, or love it for personal reasons, it's time to get rid of it.

In other words, **LOVE IT OR LOSE IT**.

Love what nourishes your dreams and directions, lose what drains or distracts you.

This book reveals a simple five-step clutter campaign proven to help people like you (and all of us) get rid of clutter and prevent clutter comeback. It also shares the real stories of people we have helped. Some people followed the five steps to produce immediate results, and others wrestled with more complex issues to eventually triumph over the clutter in their homes, workplaces and hearts.

These people found new focus and freedom, new simplicity and serenity, new energy and enlightenment in their journeys. They discovered that it is only by knowing what to let go of, that they could know more clearly what to hold on to.

One reader nicknamed the boost of extra energy he got when he started living clutter-free. He took the initials of the phrase LOVE IT OR LOSE IT and called his new feeling the LILI Factor. We've adapted his idea and used a lily logo in the layout of this book to remind you of the sense of spaciousness, ease, and freedom coming your way.

To explore how to build a clutter-free personal world of your own, and be inspired by the real stories of other people who are enjoying their own new freedom, please read on....

Living Clutter-Free Forever

TABLE OF CONTENTS

Living Clutter-Free Forever

PART I

ESCAPING THE CLUTTER TRAP

What liberty a loosened spirit brings!
Emily Dickinson

"BUT I HAVE BETTER THINGS TO DO THAN OR-GANIZE MY JUNK DRAWER."

You're busy. Yet every once in a while you feel a pang of good-intentions-that-never-get-acted-on guilt when you look at an area of your home or office that needs some attention. Before you even complete the thought, the phone rings, the email dings, and your kids call out, "Don't forget to pick us up at four o'clock sharp!"

The guilt pang is pushed aside as you say to yourself: "I like an attractive, orderly setting as much as the next person, but with everything else I have to think about right now, is it really that important? Can't it wait till I have time to get around to it?

Consider the hidden costs of clutter. A setting that is crowded, cramped, or chaotic can result in a slow drain on staying healthy, happy, and productive. It can cost you in dimensions both profound and subtle. Here are glimpses of some people who decided to eliminate that drain.

"You May Have Just Saved My Marriage."

"You may have just saved my marriage," the woman said as she talked to Barbara Hemphill privately at the end of a book-signing seminar.

LOVE IT OR LOSE IT

Startled, Barbara asked, "What do you mean?"

"Well, my husband is a packrat and it drives me crazy. He has already filled our attic, garage, storage shed; and now his stuff is invading the bedroom closet that was already crammed full. He's promised many times to clear it all out, but he never does. I was starting to think he just didn't care enough about my need to live in some degree of order and raise our children that way. I am frustrated, embarrassed, and depressed to see how we live. I'd begun to think about divorce, until something you said today."

"What was it?" Barbara invited.

"Remember when you said your setting tells the whole world secrets about your life? And that people who can't let go of things have often had a significant unresolved loss in their lives?"

"Yes, I do."

"My husband's mother died when he was four years old. I always knew that loss affected him deeply, but I never before linked it to this need to hold on to things. I want to go back and see if he'll get some help with this. I hate to give up on our marriage, and maybe I don't have to."

Living clutter-free can improve your relationships.

"I Wish I Had Done This Years Ago."

After a long intensive session of working together to organize his office, a United States ambassador told Barbara, "I should have met you years ago when my career was beginning."

"Excuse me, Mr. Ambassador, but you seem to have done very well without me."

"But you have no idea what I might have accomplished if I had not been so disorganized. My career is full of nuance and subtlety. Yet I spent way too much time distracted by details like lost papers and missing materials.

"A more organized setting would have left me free to focus on critical alliances rather than draining my attention away on administrative details. I'm glad I finally did this. I just wish I had done it sooner."

**Living clutter-free
can enhance your career.**

"My Passion Was Totally Shut Down."

"Establishing my photography business based at home was fine when I had only one child and very few clients," Susan reported. "Then my family and my company both flourished and suddenly there were David and I, two children, and a successful business operating in the same space we had started with.

"I noticed that laundry was gradually taking over from lenses. I loved our townhouse in the historic area of Alexandria, Virginia, and I had always counted on the visual stimulation of my home and community to get me inspired. But finally I found myself feeling listless, tired all the time, and tired of feeling tired. Every time I looked at kids' shoes in one corner and an abandoned toy truck in another, I just wanted to get out of there.

"The worst part for me is that I am so responsive to my environment. My setting either energizes me or drains me. I had to drag a thousand cobwebs off my brain before I could 'see' again to do my photography. It was like my passion was totally shut down and imprisoned in a smothering clutter trap."

As Susan and her family went on a drastic clutter diet, she reawakened her artistic eyes and resurrected her passion for her work.

Living clutter-free can invite your talents to flourish.

"That Day Saved Our Company From Disaster."
Another client had heard Barbara speak about her book, *Taming the Paper Tiger at Work*. The talk had focused on the theme that "top tigers have no paper," that explored the idea that the skills that make people successful leaders, entrepreneurs, and artists are the very skills that make them lousy at managing their surroundings. They have a hard time deciding how one piece of paper that makes them think of fourteen key words can be put in one file folder and found easily later.

The business owner brought Barbara in to work with him and his assistant. They spent a day organizing and indexing all the corporate documents and active files.

He called three weeks later and said, "That one day we worked together saved our company from disaster. My assistant quit unexpectedly one week later to join her fiancé who had been transferred overseas. Those indexes we created allowed me to hire a replacement and keep operating smoothly with minimal interruption of projects."

Living clutter-free can prevent disruptive disasters.

"I Resolve To Take Action Now."

Kim and her brother had just finished moving their widowed mother into senior housing less than half the size of the home the family had enjoyed for more than thirty years. The mother's health was fragile, and the move had been wrenching for everyone. The siblings had hired professional organizers to help reduce the physical and emotional toll on each of them. That helped a lot.

Later, when they were sharing hot-fudge sundaes to celebrate a successful move, Kim told her brother, "I will never let my house get cluttered with that much stuff."

"That's big talk from someone who still has her Barbie doll collection and her first Beanie Baby," her brother said.

"No, I mean it. Always until now I saw clutter as just something I'd take care of when I had enough time to get organized, or as something that I could just rearrange logically or contain attractively."

"So what's different now?" he asked.

"Now it really hits home that clutter is not just messy, inconvenient, and sometimes embarrassing. It gradually eats away at my precious space, time, and peace of mind — because something is always nagging at me. If I sit down to enjoy a quiet cup of coffee, I notice all the things that need to be put away or rearranged, and I just don't relax."

"Aw, Sis," teased her brother, "I think you just never want to burden your adult kids with having to sort through your old underwear drawer, years from now, like we just did for Mom."

LOVE IT OR LOSE IT

"You may be right. But at this moment, I'm angry with Mom for letting her house get as bad as it did. I want to head off that feeling for my own kids. So this time it really is different. Here's my new resolution:

"I am no longer willing to feel frustrated and smothered by the disorder around me. I resolve to take action now."

Living clutter-free can eliminate burdens and guilt to ensure a legacy of love.

Living clutter free can eliminate:
- Risks to relationships you value
- Distractions that rob you of focus and energy
- Blocks to your creativity and other life gifts
- Dangerous dependence on others who may not always be around
- Leaving behind an unintentional burden of resentment, guilt, or regret

HOW DID YOU GET STUCK IN A CLUTTER TRAP?

You arrived on earth without clutter. Your parents and caring relatives started you on a pathway to accumulation. By the time you were a year old, you had mounds of functional clothing, twenty outfits suitable for dress-up, too many stuffed animals, custom-sized furniture, a silver spoon, and a plastic Winnie-the-Pooh bowl. Perhaps there was also your christening gown: an heirloom already packed safely away waiting for the next generation. You had not even become a toddler yet, and you had already embarked on the road to the clutter trap.

Perhaps your most treasured possession during this time was a favorite "blankie." This was one item that just made you feel good when you dragged it everywhere you went. You also had a rattle that served two valuable functions. It made noise, and it was handy to chew on when your gums hurt. And the most attractive item in your crib area was that mobile of the shiny fish that swam above your head. Even at this early age, you were surrounded by some things you loved, some things you found useful, and some things you found beautiful.

LOVE IT OR LOSE IT

And there was other "stuff" too. There were broken toys, clothes you were rapidly outgrowing, a quilt someone made that felt scratchy. These were the beginnings of clutter in your life. But were you caught in the clutter trap?

No! You weren't trapped because you didn't care. You didn't interrupt your life's work (eating, playing, sleeping, and saying "no") to worry about any of this. Your caretakers worried about them on your behalf.

By the time you became an adult, the story was different. While you were still surrounded by clothing, toys, furniture, and heirlooms, by now you had added two hair dryers, four televisions, three telephones, a computer, a washing machine, a lawn mower, a partridge-in-a-pear-tree-decoration and other machinery for life. Friends, family and colleagues had given you gifts, paintings, china, and things you never used, and didn't particularly like. But you could never quite decide to get rid of them.

HERE COMES THE CLUTTER TRAP

Although 50 to 95 percent of your life is operating very well, and you feel successful in most areas, you sometimes:

- Feel overwhelmed when you look at your closet or the garage or attic
- Put off important things because they seem too massive to tackle in your current state of mind
- Avoid having people visit your home or office because it looks too messy
- Tremble at the thought of an audit, because you probably couldn't find supporting records
- Spend hours looking for your car insurance documents
- Get headaches, neck and back tension, or grind your teeth because you can't seem to find a place to relax anywhere
- Wonder what is wrong with you that you can't seem to stay organized
- Consider taking yet another time management course to get it all under control
- Yearn to escape to a desert island.

Here's the simple truth. Everything — *everything* — you have in your life either nourishes you or drains you. It either supports your dreams and desires or sabotages them. If too much stuff in your immediate environment drains you, you are caught in the Clutter Trap.

The Clutter Trap is a state of cumulative disorder that diminishes your physical, mental, emotional, spiritual, or financial health. It is a dangerous threat to your productivity, your prosperity, and your peace of mind. Underestimate that threat at your own peril.

The Clutter Trap is more than an occasional temporary mess you make while finishing a project or getting dinner ready. It is a multiplicity of messes. It is chronic, cumulative, chaotic, cramping, creeping disorder.

OUR FAMILY AND OUR WORLD NEED OUR BEST

Suppose you wake up tomorrow with a kindly presence whispering gently in your ear. "You are such a great person, we have decided to give you your heart's desire of the most ideal setting in which to live and work." You float half-awake with welcome visions of a sun-drenched easy chair, a penthouse office, a water view, an inviting golf course just outside, cloud-soft carpets, luxurious furniture, relaxing aromas fragrant flowers, harmonious sounds, peace, calm, and order everywhere around you, and just the right amount of stimulation to keep your juices flowing.

Then you open your eyes—and reality strikes! First, you see the exercise machine draped in yesterday's gym clothes, then the closet door you hate to open for fear of being smothered by the crushing mass of things stuffed inside, then the stack of newspapers left from last weekend, then the smudge on the wall from some mysterious source, then the carpet that could use vacuuming, and finally the torn-out travel article you read last night, as you imagined a dream vacation away from all this.

"Oh well," you say to yourself, "I'll clean up tomorrow. Meanwhile I'd better brush my teeth and get going. This is a very busy day. The clutter can't be that important."

And maybe you are seriously wrong. Maybe the clutter is enormously important.

Think back to those waking moments when you imagined the ideal setting for your life and work. Think of how you would feel, act, and respond in such a setting. Would that setting help you feel focused, vigorous, strong, talented, generous, energetic, calm, relaxed, powerful, productive, or peaceful?

Then remember how you felt when reality hit. You may have felt overwhelmed, drained, depleted, depressed, or at least discouraged.

Now picture going into your day without the clutter. Which setting inclines you toward your most satisfying results and your most nourishing relationships? How much difference could the right setting make to your ability to focus, to respond fully to all the opportunities of your day, to develop fresh solutions for the challenges you face, to return home and be a more loving partner and parent, to link with your neighbors to create a stronger sense of community?

Very few people are truly impervious to their setting. Most of us just pretend we are. We make promises to ourselves to take care of the clutter later. In the meantime, we walk around as incomplete, diminished versions of the fully resourceful, fully generous people we could be.

And our family and our world need our best. Setting matters. Freedom from clutter is not just a selfish pursuit of our own comfort or convenience. It is not just a luxury that makes our setting "nicer" or "cleaner" or "safer." That freedom also unlocks us from distraction and distress, so we can connect and contribute more abundantly to our family, our community, our world. As one client said, "Save the planet, starting in my attic!"

THE KEY TO CLUTTER FREEDOM

Here is the one simple principle that can help you escape The Clutter Trap and remain clutter-free forever:

LOVE IT OR LOSE IT.

If there is anything around you that you do not know to be useful, believe to be beautiful, or treasure for reasons of your own, get rid of it. Love it or lose it. Things you do not love have no place in your heart, and should have no place in your home or workspace. That's the LOVE IT OR LOSE IT Principle.

This book helps you put that principle to work for you as you launch a Clutter Campaign consisting of five steps. These steps are:

1. DESIGN your vision of how you want to live and work
2. ELIMINATE your excuses that undermine that vision

3. COMMIT your time to take positive action
4. SELECT your tools to match your personal organizing style
5. MAINTAIN your success and keep the process flowing

Each of the steps is expanded into six options, with accompanying examples and stories of people who have put these ideas to work. The options detail actions proven over time to bring lasting results. They are called "options" because you do not need to do every one of them each time you try to clean up or organize your home or office.

If it's the day before Thanksgiving, and you have sixteen people coming to a holiday dinner, you may want to just jump in and clean up quickly. The stories we will tell will help you see how others have used or adapted the ideas, and some of the results they created for themselves.

But if you want one comprehensive, unified strategy for transforming your environment and living clutter-free forever, all of the elements in the steps and options will work together to insure enduring success. The clutter did not arrive in one single day. It will not be gone in one single day!

The Clutter Campaign is three things – a proven process, a declaration of freedom, and a way of life:

- The PROVEN PROCESS of creating a productive environment for your life and work.
- A DECLARATION OF FREEDOM from surrounding yourself with anything that robs you of focus or function
- A WAY OF LIFE that helps you stay clutter-free forever.

The GOAL of your campaign is to create a setting where everything you are or wish to be, where everything you do or need to do, is supported by everything around you, and nothing extra weighs you down

Your focus shifts from "making things better" to making things the best they can be. The Clutter Campaign takes one basic idea as its cornerstone: **Clutter is postponed decisions**. The campaign helps you make the daily decisions that lead to a life that is clutter-free forever.

This campaign is not based on any one secret ingredient for producing instant results. Instead, it is a lifelong plan for creating a healthy, productive environment that nourishes your dreams and directions, while promoting the overall enjoyment of your life and work.

LOVE IT OR LOSE IT

As one person told us, "When the surroundings out-side me match the picture in my mind of how I want to live and work, it just makes me peaceful and relaxed, yet stimulated. It's like environmental endorphins."

YOUR CHALLENGE TODAY!

This is your moment of truth. Ask yourself what you are thinking as you are holding this book, reading these words. Are you saying to yourself:

1. *Here's a nice book. Maybe it will be fun to read, and I can get a couple of good ideas.*
2. *Someday I'll get rid of all that stuff I don't need any more and maybe this book can help me.*
3. *Now here's a book my spouse/boss/kid/sister/ friend needs.*
4. *I am seriously committed to creating the setting that supports my success.*

Your selection of one of those four answers will abso-lutely determine the value you get from these pages.

While this book may satisfy readers who are looking for inspiration or a few good ideas or tips to share with others, our primary commitment is helping those who are totally committed to positive change.

Your authors are specialists in this area. Barbara Hemphill, author of *Taming the Paper Tiger* and designer of the *24-Hour Miracle*, is an expert on organizing homes and offices. Maggie Bedrosian, author of *Life is More Than Your To-Do List*, is an expert on organizing ideas and information to generate positive results.

This book features truths that we have observed and systems we have developed in more than twenty-five years in professional organizing and executive coaching. We have devised specific solutions for many different types of people, some of whom will sound like people you know. And some will sound like you.

We've helped organize the cluttered desks of television news anchors and the overstuffed closets of the rich and recognized. We've worked with harried parents and non-profit charities. The work has also taken us from the boardrooms of giant corporations to the spare-bedroom offices of budding businesses. It has taken us to those who are resistant and reluctant. It has taken us to those who are ready and resourceful. It has taken us to those who had to first change their thinking patterns before they could change their environment.

Wherever you fall in those categories, one of us has worked with someone very much like you. And we'll share an enduring approach that has worked for all those distinctly different, yet similarly clutter-afflicted people.

While you may see this challenge of getting and staying organized as a chore, you also have the opportunity to approach it as an adventure. And yes, the adventure may require honesty, courage, energy, tenacity, and occasional flashes of humor.

The stories, strategies, and systems are all designed to help you discover the liberating freedom of escaping the clutter trap forever. You will sometimes be surprised at the simplicity and instant improvements that some solutions will bring you. You may also find yourself remembering and returning to some great ideas you used in the past and had forgotten about.

The most important foundation for lasting change is that any idea has to work for you personally. Not your boss, not your spouse or family, not some expert. You as you are — human, flawed, imperfect, overworked. Because you are also bright, unique, important, contributing, and deserving of ease and beauty in your surroundings.

Living Clutter-Free Forever

This process is not about mandating one sleek version of a perfect setting you might see featured in a model home or in the pages of a glossy magazine. It is not about imposing anyone else's taste, style, or judgment on you. It is not even about simplicity, though many people find it leading naturally in that direction. And it is not the pursuit of perfection.

It is the freedom of clarity — the clarity to identify what is useful, beautiful, and treasured. The clarity to know what you want to create (your vision), not just what you want to eliminate (your clutter). The clarity to get rid of anything that weighs you down. The clarity to **love it or lose it!**

Are you ready for the challenge?

LOVE IT OR LOSE IT

The *LOVE IT OR LOSE IT* INVENTORY

Your "setting" is the immediate physical environment
surrounding your life — the organization, style, order,
arrangement, and maintenance of the place you
live or work. This brief exercise provides a glimpse
of the importance to you of creating a
setting to support your success.
It may also offer significant clues about your
willingness to make changes.

On the number line below each of the following items,
draw a **SQUARE** around the number that reflects
where you are today. Then draw a **CIRCLE** around
the number that reflects where you would like to be.
Leave **BLANK** any item that does not apply to you
(blanks have minimal effect on your score).

Take the Inventory several times, each time focusing
on **one specific area** of your work or home setting as
you answer. (Available online at LoveItOrLoseIt.com)
1 = absolute NO   10 = absolute YES

1. My setting reflects the quality I want in my life, my work,
and my relationships.

     1   2   3   4   5   6   7   8   9   10

2. This setting helps me enjoy life or work.

     1   2   3   4   5   6   7   8   9   10

3. This setting helps me reach my goals.

1   2   3   4   5   6   7   8   9   10

4. I am pleased to invite others into my setting when I want them there.

1   2   3   4   5   6   7   8   9   10

5. I have enough space.

1   2   3   4   5   6   7   8   9   10

6. Everything I need is conveniently available.

1   2   3   4   5   6   7   8   9   10

7. Everything I need is in good working order.

1   2   3   4   5   6   7   8   9   10

8. I waste no time looking for things.

1   2   3   4   5   6   7   8   9   10

9. I am confident about my system for handling important records, addresses, contracts, and legal documents.

1   2   3   4   5   6   7   8   9   10

10. I choose to maintain this setting well, without letting its care take over my life.

1   2   3   4   5   6   7   8   9   10

11. Others who share this setting feel the same way I do.

1   2   3   4   5   6   7   8   9   10

12. No one urges me to change.

1   2   3   4   5   6   7   8   9   10

13. There is nothing in my setting that makes me feel disorganized or discouraged.

$$1 \quad 2 \quad 3 \quad 4 \quad 5 \quad 6 \quad 7 \quad 8 \quad 9 \quad 10$$

14. Everything in my setting contributes to producing my most satisfying results.

$$1 \quad 2 \quad 3 \quad 4 \quad 5 \quad 6 \quad 7 \quad 8 \quad 9 \quad 10$$

Total the numbers with Circles   _____

Total the numbers with Squares   _____

Subtract the Squares from the Circles   _____

**The resulting number total equals your
Setting Satisfaction Gap**

WHAT THE NUMBERS ARE TELLING YOU:

0 - 19   Enough of the elements in your setting support your success. The good news is that you don't have a great need to make immediate improvement. The bad news is that it may be hard to give up the good to get the very best from your setting or yourself.

20 – 40   Some of the elements in your setting interfere with consistently reaching your goals. What are you willing to do about that?

40 – 60   Your setting is sabotaging your success. Are you willing to let this disparity continue to interfere with your dreams and desires?

60+   **NOT TO WORRY!** Chances are that you are now in enough discomfort that you are poised for change!

Living Clutter-Free Forever

PART II

THE FIVE-STEP
CLUTTER CAMPAIGN

*I would not give a fig for the simplicity this side
of complexity, but I would give my life for the
simplicity on the other side of complexity.*
Oliver Wendell Holmes

STEP ONE - DESIGN YOUR VISION

I like a room you can dance in the middle of!
Mariah Burton Nelson

If Life Is A Banquet, Why Am I Still Trapped In Clutter Instead Of Enjoying The Feast?

Approaching this step, take a brief look at your opportunity and responsibility to provide yourself with a setting that fosters your highest and best experience of life's banquet.

Set change into motion as you act on the options for putting this step to work for you.

Options for taking the first step:
- Assess what your setting is like right now
- Document your current condition
- Define what you want your setting to be, exactly
- Connect to your life purpose
- Document your desired future state
- Set milestones, budget, and time frames.

LOVE IT OR LOSE IT

CLUTTER IS POSTPONED DECISIONS

Remember that one basic idea — clutter is postponed decisions. Now ask yourself if you've ever really decided what you want your setting to be. Chances are you have not thought much about this. One client described her frustration at "visiting the banquet of life and feeling stuck in the mashed potatoes — all the stuff holding me down." Only later did she define an entirely different place on life's banquet table. She wanted to feel as bright as a bowl of fresh raspberries — rich, tangy and colorful.

When you were a kid, you mostly accepted the setting that was provided for you. When you first lived on your own or with a roommate, you didn't think much about your surroundings. You were too absorbed in school, work, or socializing to focus on an ideal setting (or maybe your "ideal" environment actually did include socks on the light fixture and empty pizza boxes overflowing the wastebasket).

Eventually, you had more opportunities to create your own setting. By then maybe you were "too busy to take the time" or "too broke from moving." So somehow you ended up exactly where you are today. Are you surrounded by things you find useful, beautiful, and treasure—or are you surrounded by a blend of inherited cast-offs, family heirlooms, quirky youthful choices, and accidental or impulsive acquisitions?

Today is a perfect time to ask yourself some challenging questions. You don't need to think deeply about each of these. Pick two or three that trigger instant reactions. Share your thoughts with someone or write them down to read later after you've completed your clutter campaign.

- What setting would encourage you to make the highest and best use of all your skills and talents?
- What environment would best support your many roles in life, from parent/spouse to worker to tango dancer?
- How and where would you choose to locate and live if job, family, or money were not a factor?
- What setting would most satisfy your spirit?
- What setting would offer you the most freedom?
- What do you most NOT want in your setting?
- What setting would provide the ideal match for your most cherished dreams and directions?
- What setting would best display your values (or your valuables)?

LOVE IT OR LOSE IT

OPTIONS FOR DESIGNING YOUR VISION

OPTION 1. ASSESS WHAT YOUR SETTING IS LIKE RIGHT NOW

Have you ever noticed how much you seem not to notice about your everyday environment? Look around yourself right now and you'll probably "see" many things that have become invisible to you on a daily basis because you have trained yourself not to see them.

There are those three towering stacks of articles and newsletters you intend to read as soon as you have time. Or the star-shaped stress toy someone gave you at a meeting. Then there's that second calendar. You didn't really need another calendar; but you liked the black ebony holder it came in, so you put that on your desk too. And then there's that mug from your sister with the funny picture of her dog, and you always smile when you see that. And the warranty card for the cell phone you can't remember if you still have or not. And the pen set they gave you when you won the award last year.

Somehow all this stuff seems to have arrived on the top of your desk and you can hardly see the surface of the desk any more. You just know you can barely find any flat space to work.

The choices you make for your surroundings and environment hand the world an amazing array of clues about you. "But I don't live my life based on what other people think," you may respond. Even so, you might occasionally be surprised what your setting reveals — sometimes it reveals secrets you were keeping even from yourself. Here's a story from one client who tells about discovering her own secret. After she shared this story, we had some important clues about what this woman wanted us to help her create in her work setting.

I RECOGNIZE THE SECRETS
THE WHOLE WORLD KNOWS ABOUT ME

Peggy reports:

> *"My first year in a new community, I visited the annual House Tour. Ten of the local homes offered tours to the public as a charity fundraiser. I remember being impressed at what I saw in these lovely homes. About five years later, I got a call from the committee inviting us to show our home on the tour in the*

coming spring. 'I'm flattered to be asked, but give me a day or so to think about it.' I responded.

"I mentioned the invitation to two of my friends while I was seriously considering accepting the honor. Each of them greeted the news with one of those pauses saturated with caution. 'Your home is wonderful, Peggy, but the house tour format is that they walk through and ogle every inch of your home.' Alice observed. 'One of the women last year even decorated an extra closet as a computer station, installing an Apple computer, painting the walls apple green, and applying a red and white apple-print border. Both the host houses and the people buying tickets are deeply interested in 'themes' and 'looks' and 'vignettes.' I'm not sure you really want to invite that level of scrutiny into your home.'

"I stepped back for a moment. I never look at my house objectively, and in a single instant, I recognized that others would not see my home the way I do. I see the three-foot wooden pig planter in the corner of the foyer not as the holder of a slightly dusty silk plant, but as a jaunty reminder of a farm vacation years ago. I

see the faded family-room couch as a comfortable lounge area, scene of many great family
wrestling matches, bowls of popcorn, and
scrabble games. No scattering of bright throw
pillows would make it look entirely fresh for
objective display.

'I don't mean to say your home isn't lovely,'
another friend assured me in the kindest possible voice. 'It's just that decorating is not your
primary life focus, and you have chosen instead to focus on family, work, and friends, and
to use your considerable gifts elsewhere.'

"The minute she said that, I could see that it
was true. I had never before considered that
my home spoke so clearly of my values and
my focus, and also of the things that I don't put
too much stock in. While I am not overly con-
cerned with how others see me, it was refresh-
ing to get such a clear glimpse of the kind of
telegram I was sending to the world around
me.

"I turned down the offer to show my house,
volunteered as a guide at one of the other

LOVE IT OR LOSE IT

houses, and enjoyed pointing out the Faux-painting 'treatment' in the kitchen to all who visited.

"Once I recognized the secret I was communicating to others, I realized it was exactly the message I would choose to send. I am more focused on energy than on elegance, more on comfort than on classical styling, and more on what-you-see-is-what-you-get functionality, rather than on formality."

It's time to take an honest and unflinching look at exactly how things are at this very moment, and what telegram you want to be sending to the world. While this unflinching assessment is especially valuable in a business setting, it can also provide valuable insight into what gives you peace and pleasure at home.

This does not have to be an overwhelming task. Decide on one area you want to focus on first. This might be one closet, one desk, one countertop, one wall. Don't be too ambitious. Avoid choosing an area larger than one room.

Go to that area and assess exactly how things are now. Let the images, textures, smells, light, and sound come alive vividly in your brain. Ask yourself: "Is this setting inspiring me and supporting my ideal life?" "Is this the story I want the world to know about me?"

Ron reports,

> *"I thought I'd be really smart and pick just one drawer in the kitchen. This is the drawer that holds all the small gadgets like bottle openers and cheese slicers. How bad could one drawer be? I was amazed at the useless stuff in there. Not only was it taking up space, and offering stray kitchen crumbs a perfect hiding place, but some of it was literally dangerous. One cheese knife and server had a curved point I could easily hook an innocent finger on while reaching for my favorite bottle opener."*

Tim offers another way to take a fresh look at your surroundings.

> *"About six months ago, we decided to become a 'virtual' company. We gave up our office space, hooked up our computers, and committed to working from home. Everything seemed fine for a while. Then I scheduled two clients to*

LOVE IT OR LOSE IT

come by for a strategy session. I looked around at my den/office and at the half-bath down the hall. Suddenly, they weren't just convenient family spaces where I could work all night in a bathrobe, and leave a half-empty yogurt container on the desk. Now I noticed the drooping wallpaper trim and the magazines cascading onto the floor.

"The setting that had seemed fine when I was working there alone now seemed cluttered and confining as I looked at it with the imagined eyes of my clients. Having an occasion to see the area with new eyes was a giant step toward improving it."

OPTION 2. DOCUMENT YOUR CURRENT CONDITION

Now it's time for the *before* pictures. Get a camera or video and capture images of the area without a single change. Or you might draw a sketch, make a list of the contents, or do a funny audiotape like broadcaster describing the layout of an old museum.

The goal of this activity is two-fold. First, it gives you a progress-marker to revisit later to see how far you've come. (You will probably forget how bad it was.)

Second, as you do this in several areas of your environment, you may start to see clues to a repeating clutter profile. The clues can then suggest ideas for developing more productive patterns for the future.

I WAS GLAD I'D INVITED
AN OUTSIDE OBSERVER

Karen reports:

"I came to this exercise reluctantly, thinking it a waste of time. 'Why not just get on with cleaning up?' I thought. I even imagined I'd fling a few things around to make the clutter more dramatic, and therefore feel later that I'd accomplished more.

"I was laughing as I took pictures of my home office. I had gotten so good at denial that I didn't realize I had overflowing boxes stacked under my desk where I pretended no one could see them. I had been bumping into those boxes for months and pretending they weren't there. I also realized my desktop held a candy jar that offered way too many snacking temptations. It's amazing what I was pretending not to see.

LOVE IT OR LOSE IT

"I knew I'd need help with this step. I don't seem to have the gift of being objective about my own setting. So I asked a close friend to help me. She's a gifted real estate agent, and she herself had recently moved and had done some remodeling. I asked her to come by for dinner one evening, walk through the whole house with me, and give me her best advice. 'Pretend I'm a client listing my house with you, and I want it to sell quickly.' I told her. 'What are all the distractors I might get rid of to make the house show better?' I knew I might get defensive at some of her comments, so I audiotaped her analysis as we walked through the house.

"She took to the task almost too eagerly. Maybe these were things she had been wanting to tell me for years. I thanked her for her help and listened to the tape two or three times in the car that week as I was driving. I agreed with almost everything she said.

"She complimented me later saying, 'It makes me sad sometimes that so many people wait till they are ready to move to look closely at their setting. Then they finally make the changes that might have helped them enjoy their home more while they lived there.'

Living Clutter-Free Forever

"I was glad I'd invited an outside expert ob-server, and glad also that I had taped her comments. The tape helped me absorb her advice over several days, and to be more neutral about what I was hearing."

OPTION 3. DEFINE WHAT YOU WANT YOUR SETTING TO BE, EXACTLY

This is a valuable exercise and one many people imagine they can easily skip. You may be thinking, "I just want it cleaned up, cleared off, and efficient." That may be "good enough for now," but it isn't the best that is possible.

This is the time for total and completely luxurious honesty. Ask yourself, what setting would encourage you to operate to your highest and best purpose on earth?

What colors, textures, tools, light, air, furniture, fixtures, sounds, and aromas would help you to concentrate, dream, and perform?

Actor Jeremy Irons played twin gynecologists in the 1988 film, *Dead Ringers*. One twin was amiable and one was evil. Irons knew how much focus and concentration he would need to bring subtle differences

LOVE IT OR LOSE IT

to each character. He wanted to play them absolutely distinctly for each scene, and never let even a single mannerism spill over from one brother to the other.

One element of his solution was to insist on two dressing rooms, each carefully decorated and outfitted to match the character and behavior of the separate personalities. Before appearing in each scene, he would spend time in the room matching the character he was about to play. His performance was flawless.

Your performance, too, derives in part from your setting. It becomes a circle. Character becomes setting becomes character.

I DISCOVERED I COULD MAKE MYSELF HAPPIER AT WORK

Mary tells her own story:

> *"I never imagined that I could define a dream environment, because I always felt I had so little control of my setting. I work with second graders, and everything is designed for safety, cleanliness, and the height of children.*
>
> *"Then one day, a neighbor was finishing up her yard sale. She called over to me across the*

driveway. 'Mary, would you like any of this stuff for your classroom? I'd be happy to donate anything you want to cart away.' I selected two of the items – a carpet with numbers printed on large squares and a child's musical keyboard. I took them both into school and designed some learning games for each that my kids could do in their free time. I was pleased that one for-merly reluctant learner would finish his worksheets just to earn time on the keyboard.

"The bigger surprise, though, was that these yard-sale items and a little creativity could help make me happier at work. I started setting aside ten dollars and one Saturday morning a month to search for similar treasures at local yard sales. Another teacher joined me, and we turned the enterprise into a treasure hunt. Sometimes we found no treasures, but we had a great visit, and once or twice we went over our budgets.

"It didn't take long before we realized we could turn our classrooms into clutter traps too. So one Saturday, we skipped the yard sales, and went to our school to draw diagrams and floorplans of our classrooms. We sketched the desks, furniture, and learning stations. Then we

LOVE IT OR LOSE IT

did something I'd never done before for any of the settings in my life. We sat down at a neighborhood cafe, and talked about our ideal settings.

"This was the most engaged I had ever felt in designing my working environment. And it felt good. We still went back to yard-sale bargain hunting. But finally, and for the first time in my life, I was operating from a picture of what I wanted, rather than from an impulse of the moment or a circumstance of the marketplace."

Sheryl had a different proactive approach when she was assigned a small inside office with no window.

She went to a hardware store and bought a standard sash double-hung window. She mounted a landscape poster behind it, hung it on her office wall, added a sheer window treatment and enjoyed the new 'openness' of her small space.

OPTION 4. CONNECT TO YOUR LIFE PURPOSE

Why are you sitting or standing exactly where you are right this moment? Chances are your answer, if you attempted one at all, would be a wandering essay on your life patterns that led you to this desk, chair, or beach blanket beside the ocean.

It almost doesn't matter. You are today the sum total of all your thoughts, dreams, and actions, every chili dog you ever ate, every joke you ever laughed at, every sunset you ever enjoyed. If you are just over 27 years old, you have been on earth 10,000 days. At just over 54, 20,000 days. At 81, 30,000. What's the point here? Maybe this is a good time to define or revisit your purpose and patterns in life.

"Isn't this a lofty detour on the path to cleaning out my garage?" one client asked. Then we went back to those four simple words. Clutter is postponed decisions. Once you know your purpose, your decisions can be more swift and sure. Otherwise, your garage becomes a home to all the stuff you may just be holding in reserve in case it happens to match your purpose - if you could someday figure out what that was. You deserve better.

Clarity of purpose brings clarity about what to keep and what to throw away.

What follows is one person's adventure with creating a purpose statement.

LOVE IT OR LOSE IT

I AM MY OWN LIGHTKEEPER

Maggie reports:

"A speaker I heard at a conference a few years back really prompted me to do some fresh thinking. He told us the entire purpose of his life in about 20 words. I could hear in his voice that he was telling a bedrock truth. This statement reflected his essence, his reason for being on earth right now with his own particular set of skills, resources, and experiences. I don't remember his statement. What I remember clearly is that he had defined for himself a nugget of certainty in an uncertain world. And he inspired me to do the same.

"Since the statement was supposed to be a very few words, I figured I'd have it done in a day or so. I was so wrong. My first try was about two hundred words long, and it didn't seem to say enough to crystallize my life purpose. So I made it longer. The next version was about six hundred words, and it seemed to include most everything I wanted. But I would not remember to think of it to start each day, or to sort out tough choices. I started cutting.

"It took me about six months to get the statement down under 25 words. I knew I wanted some word in there that referred to 'light.' I thought it would be a word like 'sparkle,' or 'dazzle.' But every statement I wrote with those supercharged words just made me feel tired. And I knew that my true purpose statement would make me feel uplifted, never tired. Finally I found the perfect word. 'Glow.' I finally had a ten-word statement that became my touchstone, my basis for testing the value of each element in my life. My purpose is:

**To glow with life and learning
and invite others along.**

"I've been using my purpose statement for several years now to help sort through business and personal choices. Finally it dawned on me it could also help cut clutter. I picture the 'glow' in my statement as a strong and steadfast light, but one that can be blocked by too much stuff trying to smother it. I am my own lightkeeper and part of my job is to keep that light from getting blocked.

"Seeing how important that responsibility is sometimes heartens my campaign against clutter when I am tempted to give up."

LOVE IT OR LOSE IT

OPTION 5. DOCUMENT YOUR DESIRED FUTURE STATE

Finally, here's an option you can skip if you want to, without great risk. But it does offer some powerful benefits, especially if you are working on a space you share with other people, or if you are enlisting the help of family or friends in your pursuit of an ideal setting.

This option invites you to create a two- or three-dimensional model of what you have in mind for an outcome. Your model can be in written or pictorial form, can be a floorplan with dimensions, pictures, magazine cutouts, paint samples, fabric swatches, and any other details you can specify. You can even make it with toothpicks.

The goal here is to get the image from inside your head to show up in concrete form outside your head. You can then use this objective model in several ways.

- To evaluate that this does indeed please you as much as you had imagined
- To gather the elements or products you need to make your vision a reality
- To communicate your vision to others and avoid misunderstandings.

I WANTED ONE WALL TO SING
WITH BRIGHT COLOR

Jan reports:

"I knew I was in trouble when I told my husband I wanted to paint one wall in the foyer. He just didn't get it when I told him I wanted the wall to 'sing with bright red color.' He brought home some paint color sample strips that were an ugly cross between eggplant and maroon. I went to the store and found a color closer to what I wanted. He was very skeptical of my choice.

"Painting the wall was only one small but important part of my clutter-free campaign. Even so, I did not want to alienate my best volunteer partner.

"I took the time to cut some photos out of magazines and to draw a floor plan. This 'model' illustrated how the new wall color and our current sofa table could create a welcoming entry station into our home and also serve as a spot for keys and incoming mail.

LOVE IT OR LOSE IT

"My husband made a couple of suggestions, which I was able to incorporate. My sister visited from out of town during this time, viewed my model, and offered a good idea about using one particular basket to hold the mail.

"It was especially heartening when my sister and I spent a day on the town and came home amazed to find the wall painted the perfect red. My husband had gained such confidence from the model I made that he painted it as a surprise.

"I'm honestly not sure I would do this step if I only had to please myself, but it sure brought good results in this case."

OPTION 6. SET MILESTONES, BUDGET, AND TIME FRAMES

This option is a joy for two types of people. First, those who like to know up front approximately how much time and money this project will consume, and second, those who need to know that at some point, it will be over — and they can celebrate.

The bad news is that it's never really over. The good news is that there is much to celebrate along the way.

Just as work expands to fill the time allowed, this process can become a drudgery that eats your life. So here's a helpful thought. Imagine you have a few good friends coming over for dinner. There's so much you'd like to do before they arrive. You prepare the food, select the music, make sure the guest bath is presentable, and start toward the sofa to fluff the pillows. As you are walking across the room, the doorbell rings. Darn, your guests are exactly on time. You forget about the fluffing, greet your guests, and enjoy a fine evening. If they had arrived a full hour later, you might easily have continued doing "just one more thing" until they rang your bell.

It's your *life* ringing that doorbell. You can keep fluffing those pillows forever, or you can start the music, answer the door, and enjoy the occasion.

So the purpose of this option is to know when to stop, pause, rest, relax, and start again another time.

LOVE IT OR LOSE IT

I TACKLE PROBLEMS, KNOWING
THEY HAVE AN END POINT

Nick shares one idea that worked for him:

"Whenever I'm frustrated by something on the computer, I set this little timer on my watch for fourteen minutes. I figure that's how much patience I have. Fifteen minutes might drive me crazy, but I can handle anything for fourteen minutes. Then I tackle the problem, knowing there is an end point. I keep my mind clear, instead of letting my frustration take over. If I can't solve the problem in fourteen minutes, I take a break or call a friend for help.

"One day I had to clean out the garage, and make some storage space for the martial arts trophies we needed to move out of the brand-new nursery. It hit me. Why not invent a sporting event with timed intervals to tackle this job? I gave myself four 'quarters' of 22 minutes and 22 seconds each. That's the easiest number to enter on my kitchen timer. I just hit the same number four times and tapped 'start.'

"After the first four quarters, I had to go into 'overtime play' for another three quarters. Finally, I decided it was time for a beer break, since I had played such an impressive game.

"It's not going to get me on 'ESPN Sports Center' anytime soon, but it was a fun fantasy for a former college jock, now the big-time dad of an infant daughter."

STEP TWO - ELIMINATE YOUR EXCUSES

Clutter is dandruff on the shoulders of your room.
Christopher Lowell

You're The One Who Invented Them Anyway.

Approaching step two, take a brief look at the most common barriers and excuses that keep people trapped in clutter.

Then continue your positive changes as you act on the following options.

Options for taking the second step:

- Let go of any excuses today
- Recognize your right to claim this freedom
- Embrace your opportunity and responsibility to affect your environment
- Banish guilt, fear, and resentment
- Tap your natural source of organizing energy
- Observe the successes of others.

YOU HAVE TO SEE THE BARRIERS BEFORE YOU CAN BREAK THROUGH THEM!

The most dangerous barriers that trap you are the ones you don't even see. What is it that prevents you from enjoying an ideal setting? If you are like most people, you'll say one of five things:

- I just don't have the time to keep it all organized.
- There's no room to put everything, so it just piles up everywhere.
- It wouldn't make any difference if I cut my clutter because it would all be back again next week.
- This isn't all my stuff. A lot of it belongs to the kids, the dog, the Boy Scouts, or my spouse.
- You never know when something might come in handy. I just know that the minute I get rid of it I'll probably need it.

As long as you have excuses, you'll have clutter. As long as you have clutter, you'll have excuses. Isn't it time to let go of both?

OPTIONS FOR ELIMINATING EXCUSES

OPTION 1. LET GO OF YOUR EXCUSES TODAY

The big excuses boil down to this:

- *No time*
- *No hope*
- *No space*
- *It's not my fault*
- *It may come in handy someday.*

The variations on these are creative and nearly infinite:

- *If we get rid of the old computer, sure enough the new one will crash, so let's keep it nearby for a few months.*
- *What if I leave our custom-tailored drapes behind when we move, and we buy another place just like this one?*
- *This clutter is only till I get my project done. Then it will all disappear.*
- *Those darn kids leave their sports equipment all over the house.*
- *I'll get organized as soon as we get the new bookcases.*
- *I promise I'll get around to it this weekend.*

Living Clutter-Free Forever

Letting go of excuses involves a courageous mental gymnastic maneuver. You move your mind from thinking "I can't because..." to thinking "I will because..."

- *I will because I'm worth it.*
- *I will because I operate better in orderly and harmonious surroundings.*
- *I will because I like never losing things to clutter.*
- *I will because I am committed to living in a setting where everything I am, or wish to be, is supported by everything around me.*

MOST OF MY EXCUSES
WERE SHEER PROCRASTINATION

Kate tells her story:

> *"Growing up, I had to share a room with my kid sister. There was one great thing about that. I could blame everything on her, and our parents would give up on us, because we made it too difficult to hold both of us accountable. In college, I had a roommate to blame things on. In my first apartment, I had two roommates to blame. So I could almost assure myself that there was nothing overly sloppy about me. Then, I got a promotion and moved into my own office for the first time.*

"At first, I was fairly organized. Then I had an assistant for a while who was a big help. Naturally, he got pulled off for other assignments when we got really busy, and I was on my own. After about two months I was tearing my hair out. I couldn't find things. I held all my client meetings in the conference room, because my office was a disaster. I'd try to work and just felt frustrated and distracted by everything around me. I started having jaw problems from grinding my teeth, and my perpetual fantasy was that someone would appear and massage the knots out of my neck and shoulders.

"About the fifth time I complained to a friend at lunch, she hit me with a hard question. 'What are you waiting for?' I told her didn't know what she meant. 'I mean you keep complaining, but you don't do anything. Do you think the Clutter Fairy is going to come rescue you? Do you think your mom will clean it all up? Do you think your assistant will come back? Why are you procrastinating? Why don't you stop complaining and stalling and do something about it?'

"She was right. I was waiting for help. Or waiting to be less busy. Or waiting for a new

system. I finally had to say to myself, 'This is a problem now. This problem is threatening my health and my ability to produce results. This problem is not going to go away if I keep stalling. In fact, it will get worse. I have to stop the waiting and face the challenge.'

It was very difficult to accept that reality. But for me, it was the most powerful step in creating my setting for success."

OPTION 2. RECOGNIZE YOUR RIGHT TO CLAIM THIS FREEDOM

Some of your clutter accumulates because you are putting other people's needs ahead of your own. You let your kids store stuff in your garage, because their apartment is so small. You keep the boxes of archives for the community history project, because nobody else considers them important. You have a closet full of things for the charity drive, because collection has just been postponed six months. Your attic is full of "treasures" from your in-laws' estate, because your children might want them one day.

When such choices are made freely and space is abundant, these may be wise and generous gestures. When they intrude on your own flexibility or peace-of-mind, you have every right to say "No!" You do not owe square footage to anyone else. You do not have to agree to store anything for anyone. Period.

I WAS NOT DOING
EITHER OF US A FAVOR

Adrienne reports:

"When my daughter moved into a smaller apartment, she asked if I would house her collection of exotic house plants 'temporarily.' She also wanted to store all her seasonal and holiday decorations in a big box in the garage. The decorations were no problem. But the plants started to take over my life. They required watering, feeding, special lighting, and dusting on a regular basis. And then my daughter would come by for a visit and criticize my caretaking efforts.

"I was invited to a conference overseas and was scheduled to be away for two weeks. Instead of being pleased for me about the career opportunity, my daughter's first reaction was, 'Who will you get to take care of the plants?' I knew that things had gone too far.

"I invited her over for dinner and suggested she select one or two favorite plants and take them home that very night. I gave her three weeks to find homes for the rest of the plants—after which I would offer them to my friends for adoption.

"She complied, a bit reluctantly. Today we respect each other more than ever and 'plant nagging' is absent from our visits. I see now that my desire to be kind and accommodating to her needs, while ignoring my own, was not doing either of us a favor. I now take more responsibility for setting boundaries that keep me from feeling like a pushover, while maintaining a better balance in family relationships."

OPTION 3. EMBRACE YOUR OPPORTUNITY AND RESPONSIBILITY TO AFFECT YOUR ENVIRONMENT

A colleague made an alarming statement the other day. "I guess I'm just a natural-born slob and I'll never get any better," he said.

Do you think this man will ever escape his clutter trap? Not as long as he denies any responsibility for it. And not as long as he considers his helplessness somehow "just-the-way-it-is."

You do have a responsibility to affect your environment, and it's simply not wise to avoid it.

Now imagine this passive, accepting spirit permeating an entire organization. We worked with a company in the northeast that prided itself on its hundred-year history. They were good people with an excellent product. The snag was that they were still keeping handwritten records. When the file cabinets got full, the records were moved to boxes. The boxes were labeled and stacked in storerooms. When space ran out, the boxes crept out to line one wall of the entrance hallway. Then they spilled over into the lobby to greet clients and visitors. "It was almost like working in a setting designed by Charles Dickens," one person commented. Most paralyzing of all, there was even an air of venerable tradition (or reluctant resignation) about the whole thing. "That's just how we do things here," was a typical comment.

When the new CEO arrived last year, there were more than 840 boxes stacked here and there. He made a very clear pronouncement. "This is *not* how we do things here anymore." In consultation with a strategy committee, he developed guidelines on what to keep and what to throw away. All the staff joined in for an eight-day purge of old records.

The staff now prides itself that their venerable tradition lives on in the quality of their product and service — and not in the Victorian eccentricity of their paperwork.

There are many opportunities to affect a change in your environment. A change in leadership (as we saw in this story), a move, a remodeling, or a shift in circumstances. Sometimes it's a radical shift, as this story illustrates.

FROM 25,000 CUBIC FEET TO 100 CUBIC FEET FOR 110 DAYS

Maggie reports:

> "My husband had just retired, and I was in a work slowdown that I hoped was temporary. We had faced these slowdowns before, and we had learned an important principle. Work comes back; money comes back; time never comes back. So we resolved to use this unexpected gift of time to drive cross-country.

"One strong attraction was that our first grand-child was due to be born in a few months. The baby's parents were on the West Coast and we were on the East Coast, so our destination was an easy choice. Knowing that babies are sometimes not on schedule, we wanted the maximum flexibility for our arrival date, and we needed cheap but comfortable lodging. We hadn't been camping in nineteen years, and we'd never been winter camping; but we were open for adventure.

"We fitted out the back of our minivan with a custom platform bed structure 27 inches off the floor. (This still left height for us to sit up in bed at night to read.) There were compartments under the bed for clothes and gear. A fluffy down comforter would keep us toasty warm on cold winter nights. We were looking forward to the novelty of such small but cozy quarters, and to the freedom to overnight in national parks and campgrounds right beside the Pacific.

"In the weeks before we left, I found myself occasionally looking around our house and cherishing the height of the ceilings and loving the tallness of our furniture. It dawned on me *that I had always thought of us as living in a house of 2,200 square feet. But now I realized that we actually live in a three-dimensional space of about 25,000 cubic feet. That's a lot of space. And now we were moving into 100 cubic feet.*

"We packed very carefully for this transition. We took our lantern, our one-burner stove, a bounty of books to read, and some basic essentials. We consciously avoided clutter. Even so, we found that we had packed too many things, 'just in case.'

"Sarah-Anne arrived on earth five weeks early, tiny but healthy. We got to meet her when she was nine days old. That was the major highlight of the trip. We spent 110 nights on the road, almost forty of them camping. The eye-opener for both of us was how comfortable we could be with so little (which was actually quite a lot).

"We came back resolved to continue some of our daily disciplines at home. It doesn't work entirely, but we certainly got a new perspective on embracing an opportunity to shape our setting."

OPTION 4. BANISH FEAR AND GUILT

It's time for another brain-check. How much does fear or guilt contribute to your clutter? The antidote to fear is knowledge. The antidote to guilt is wisdom.

The knowledge you need to overcome fear includes clear, definite guidelines on what items you must keep for legal or medical security. Items on this list range from recent tax records to current insurance documents to an updated emergency first-aid kit and fire extinguisher.

How do you gain the wisdom to let go of guilt? Start with recognizing what you feel guilty about:

- Do you feel guilty because your setting is a total clutter trap? If so, that guilt is part of what keeps you in the trap. Wisdom offers you an escape. Invite yourself to come into your setting for 24 hours of organizing time while feeling free of guilt. Imagine you are spending the day doing a favor for someone you care about. Each item you touch carries only its own weight, with no additional reverberations scolding that, "You should have gotten rid of this long ago," or, "Don't throw me out. You may need me some day."

- Do you feel any guilt because the condition of your setting fails to support your dreams and directions? If so, wisdom might whisper to you to revisit those dreams, make them more clear, and palpable. See if nagging guilt can be subdued by the magnetic pull of a new, more powerful vision.

FINALLY I ASKED MYSELF
A BETTER QUESTION

Sally reports:

> *"We lived with my in-laws the last couple of years before they died. My mother-in-law left behind some medium-good dishes. They have a floral print with gold detailing on each piece. They sat in my kitchen cabinet and caused occasional friction between my husband and me.*

> *"He seemed to have no sentimental attachment to them and sometimes asked in a very practical way, 'If they are sitting there in our kitchen, why don't we use them casually and toss them in the dishwasher with the other dishes?'*

> *"'I'm afraid of ruining the gold trim,' I protested.*

"'If we're not using them anyway,' he reasoned, 'what difference does it make if we use them and eventually throw them away?'

"I knew he had a point, but I'd feel too guilty abusing something my mother-in-law had cared for. So the dishes were too inconvenient to use, too significant to abuse, and they sat in our crowded cupboard taking up space and occasionally triggering tension.

"Finally I asked myself a better question. 'What would be an elegant answer to this dilemma?' I asked both of us, 'How would we feel if the dishes went to another family member who cared about them?' We realized that this solution would be agreeable to both of us. Alex, 16, the great-granddaughter, said she would love to have them.

"We bubble-wrapped every piece. We packaged them with copies of old photos and some written recollections of some of the typical family gatherings and everyday meals these plates had probably witnessed. We hope she'll enjoy reading those recollections when she is older and setting up a home of her own.

"Now I'm free of the occasional pang of guilt that used to hover in my cupboard. And there are so many legacies besides dishes to remind me of my queenly mother-in-law."

OPTION 5. TAP YOUR NATURAL SOURCE OF ORGANIZING ENERGY

One excuse for staying clutter-trapped is, "but I'm not good at being organized." Rather than focusing on the excuse that you have no talents for organizing, consider emphasizing the talents you do have. Each one of us has some particular gifts in this area. One smart strategy is to identify and harness those gifts. Which of the following is true about you?

- I like to get things clean. I'll empty a shelf or spice rack regularly and take pleasure in cleaning out the area and putting things back neatly.
- My best time is early in the morning (or late at night). That's when I have lots of energy and focus. I can usually accomplish anything I work on during this peak time.
- I'm good at delegating. I define very specific outcomes, and let a qualified helper get it done. All I care about is the results.
- I keep all the right tools in a kit in the closet. When I need to freshen up an area, I don't waste any

LOVE IT OR LOSE IT

time collecting the glass cleaner from one place and the paper towels from another.

- I'm the genetic opposite of a packrat. I throw everything away. I can even get in trouble for getting rid of things I later want again. But I'd rather face the inconvenience of replacing something I decide I do want, than storing thousands of things I'll never use.
- I'm not so focused on deep cleaning, but I like to keep my area looking orderly. Things just work better for me that way. If I straighten up every day, it doesn't take long at all to keep things in shape.

Each of the statements above reflects a gift you may not even be aware of:
- Pleasure in accomplishment
- Daily energy peaks
- Delegation skills
- Being organized to stay organized
- Predisposition to clutter-freedom
- Daily discipline.

Find the one or two that apply to you, and see how your natural gifts can work even more in your favor. For example, schedule your toughest jobs for your daily energy peak times, or recall times when you employed your gifts and operated with exceptional clarity or results.

One woman reported that she had cultivated many excuses for staying disorganized, but that everything changed when a special demand called for her best.

I WAS TERROR STRUCK

Sarah reports:

> "When I inherited the responsibility for getting out my firm's annual report, I was terror struck. For the first time in my life, I knew that my work was critically important to the whole organization. Believe me, I found ways to get well organized for that job every year.

> "A few years later, when my first baby was born, I had to put those same organizing skills to work to assemble and maintain her changing table and travel bag. Everything had to be fresh, clean, and available to grab with one hand while the other hand was managing a squirming baby. I guess my own natural source of organizing energy comes from a combination of huge responsibility and fear of the consequences of messing up. I still have big gaps in my skills, but I know I can do it when I really need to."

Another idea is to barter some time from your gift with someone who is strong in a different area.

A BIG TASK GOES MORE SMOOTHLY IF I'M SHARING ENERGY WITH OTHERS

Cindy reports:

"I'm at the stage in life where I love my daily rituals. I love to set aside time for exercise, my morning coffee, and dinner with my family at least four nights a week. When I was younger, I thought routine would be a dreaded, boring enemy. Now it is my welcome friend.

"Even so, I have a fairly healthy sense of adventure. So when a friend suggested that three of us play 'helper-for-a-day,' I elected to play along. We set aside three Saturdays in July. Each of us would take turns being the 'customer' for one day. The customer was royalty for the day. She could request her two loyal helpers to do any tasks, chores, or favors from 10 A.M. to 5 P.M. on their selected Saturday.

"Hilda went first. She commissioned us to help her restore order from after her neighborhood's 4th of July picnic she had chaired. First, she started us off with fresh fruit and coffee. From

that point on, we worked all day as a relaxed, yet focused, team. We took down all the signs, packed the decorations, and returned casserole dishes from the potluck buffet. The decorations were stored away, neatly labeled. We even had time to update the community directory database with corrections people had turned in. We finished those tasks about 3:30, so we went to a nearby gift shop and helped Hilda select some half-price decorations for next year's event. 'I do feel like royalty,' she smiled. 'This has never gone so smoothly before.'

"Diane took the next Saturday because it was her son's 8th birthday party. She had her loyal team of two helpers doing party preparation while she took the group of eight boys to a morning showing of a classic 'Harry Potter' movie at a downtown theatre. They came back to a birthday-decorated house about 1 PM and we got the kids involved in preparing their own lunch banquet, including several dishes made with magic potions just like in the movie.

"The boys left about three. We cleaned up, took the party photos over for one-hour developing, did the family grocery shopping for the coming

LOVE IT OR LOSE IT

*week, picked up the pictures, and delivered
everything back to the birthday house. Diane
commented, 'I felt like one of the kids. It was so
much fun to have all the details taken care of,
and to enjoy my son's birthday with him.'*

*"Finally it was my day. I got completely away
from their 'party themes' and got help with
clutter cleanup. I decided to work on something
that had been nagging me for years—organizing more than forty years of photographs. First,
I had my team of helpers take care of my
Saturday chores for about an hour, because I
knew that would free my mind to focus for the
rest of the day. While they were out, I went
through the house, gathering individual or
batches of photos from shelves, closets, draw-
ers, files, and shoeboxes. I probably collected
more than 3,000 photos. I stacked them on
cleared-off kitchen counters, and left the dining
room area clear for sorting them into stacks.
We had a labeled area for every year since
1975, and spots on the floor for 1970-1975,
1960-1969, 1950-1959, and one pile for anything before 1950.*

*"At first I feared that friends might not be able
to help, but they proved to be better detectives*

than I had imagined. Many of the photos were in clumps from around the same date. Many had dates stamped or written on the back. My friends were good at spotting similar hairstyles, clothing, kids' ages, or body shapes. Yes, they laughed at my pregnancy photos.

"By 4 PM, we had done a basic sorting through the whole pile. I had found a few treasures to set aside and frame immediately. Some of the pictures would be perfect as part of my brother's 50th birthday celebration approaching soon. I set packets aside for each of the kids, and for special friends or family. That still left a monster pile of memories I could not deal with in one day. I packed and labeled each batch to work on later. It felt wonderful to get even this far.

"I learned once again that a big task goes much more smoothly if I'm sharing energy with friends who are talented and dedicated helpers. I also learned that the same errands I do regularly can be less stressful to do occasionally for someone else. Maybe we'll do this again next year."

LOVE IT OR LOSE IT

OPTION 6. OBSERVE THE SUCCESSES OF OTHERS

Humans are a quirky species. We want to know that we are not alone in feeling trapped by our clutter, the uncomfortable secret in our otherwise successful lives. Yet we also somehow believe our own situation to be unique.

The people we see around us all seem to be living productive lives, reasonably free of clutter. So we hesitate to admit we may need help. Most professional organizers report that people lean close and whisper in confiding details of their clutter trap. And clients often hide the severity of their clutter problem, as if organizers will not see the truth when they start to work together.

So let's be clear right now:
1. You are not alone.
2. It is perfectly natural to feel stressed.
3. You are not in the worst clutter trap in the world. The poor soul who is in that trap probably hasn't been heard from in several years.

So one of the excuses for letting clutter stay in your life is that the situation is "hopeless" and you can never escape the clutter trap. Option Six reminds you that everybody wrestles with this challenge, and people are regularly coming up with solutions. Why not learn some great strategies by watching people around you? What do they do that works for them to either cure or prevent clutter? How might you adapt their methods for your own life?

Here's a story about an unusual approach to preventing clutter after celebrating birthdays and holidays. This particular clutter-prevention strategy works in both the physical world and in the fiscal world.

GIVING THE THOUGHT
THAT GOES WITH THE GIFT

Carolyn reports:

> *"'I want to find something totally extravagant that I have no intention of buying.' I announced, making my unusually clear request to the jewelry shop clerk. The shop was not busy that Monday morning in early December on the Mississippi coast. The Thanksgiving crowd of travelers was gone, and the holiday crowds hadn't started arriving yet at the resort. The off-season lull led to inexpensive room rates and clerks who could indulge a customer like me with my strange request. The clerk,*

LOVE IT OR LOSE IT

nametagged 'Lydia', was especially accommodating and possibly even intrigued.

"'And who is this item for?' she asked.

"'It's sort of for my daughter, Brenda.' I responded. 'See, a couple of generations of two
families are here celebrating a special birthday,
and we drew names to find an especially
appropriate gift for each other.'

"'But you're not going to buy the gift?' asked
Lydia, still trying to puzzle out the request.

"'No, that's the whole idea. We all promised
each other that spending this time together
was the real gift, and that we wouldn't go crazy
with presents this year. So we are selecting the
gift, showing the receiver the gift and express-
ing the warm thoughts that each gift represents.'

"'Still, you ARE shopping, so let me help you
make your selection,' said Lydia, a gem of a
professional.

"'Well, it's kind of fun to see what people might
select for one another. Not all of us know each

other too well. I was lucky. I drew my daughter's name and I know her taste.'

"'So,' Lydia clarified, 'no credit card bills, no wrapping, no exchanges, no long lists, no shipping. Just one item from anyplace in the resort for the person whose name you drew, is that it?'

"'That's exactly right,' I beamed.

"'This is sure unusual, but it might be fun. Let's see what we can find for your daughter.' Lydia led me toward a selection of jewelry. We huddled together as I selected the perfect gift.

"That night after the birthday dinner, our group walked back to the hotel and used our after-dinner strolling time to give our gifts to one another. I brought the group into the jewelry store and asked to see the gift Lydia had put aside for my daughter. With a mixture of southern warmth and Hollywood drama, the manager unlocked the case, took out a black velvet box and opened it. In the box rested a $29,000 diamond ring, a brilliant solitaire in a Tiffany setting. She took out the ring, polished the stone one last time, and placed it on Brenda's finger.

"Brenda might have been born to model jewelry. Taken with the moment, she extended her palm toward the far wall for us to admire the exquisite fire of the ring she wore. We fell into a natural, reverent hush. Then Brenda smiled, removed the ring, and handed it back to the store manager who returned it safely to its box and case. Brenda gave me a warm hug of thanks.

"The strolling and gifting continued through the resort. The ring was the only 'gift' that came from a shop. The person who loves reading was 'given' a buttery-soft leather chair from the sports bar. One of the husbands was 'given' the monster-screen television from the same bar. The career sister was 'given' weekly spa visits for a year to reduce her tension. One of the kids was 'given' 24 hours to play on any of the games or computers in the electronic cafe.

"Every gift was accompanied with a story of appreciation about why this gift so perfectly suited the receiver. The stories were funny and fond. I have to admit, it was gifts without guilt, *and an unforgettable evening that left an afterglow of shared memories, instead of credit card bills to pay later."*

STEP THREE - COMMIT YOUR TIME

Enough is as good as a feast.
Old Irish saying

Decide When And Where To Start

Approaching this step, decide when and where to start making a significant difference in your surroundings.

Options for taking the third step:

- Reclaim the time you spend looking for things
- Track the actual time organizing takes
- Break projects into bite-sized pieces
- Schedule a Marathon Mania
- Hire a professional
- Exchange services

DECIDING TO START NOW

Decide when and where to start. You have the same amount of time each day as did Thomas Jefferson, Einstein, and Mae West. It's all in where you choose to focus your attention.

If you still catch yourself thinking, "This will never work," or, "I'll never succeed," you are right.

If, however, you can focus on three liberating words, you are closer to your clutter-free future. Those words are:

FROM NOW ON...

It all starts now. From this very moment you commit to:

- Sort today's mail as it arrives, instead of stacking it in a pile till later
- Question every new purchase to be sure it deserves space in your life
- Hold to the vision of your ideal environment and reject any excess that intrudes.

Focus first on today. Don't let another thing in your door without choosing to do so. Once you have stemmed the tide of "stuff" flowing in, you will have more time to go back and clear out the past accumulation. Recognize that this campaign against clutter will have setbacks. And get up again the next day and say to yourself, "From now on...."

The now is always new.

Start now.

OPTIONS FOR COMMITTING YOUR TIME

OPTION 1. RECLAIM THE TIME YOU SPEND LOOKING FOR THINGS

So where will you find the time to take the actions recommended in this book? What if you never had to look for anything again? What if the scissors, stamps, keys, or measuring spoons were instantly available when needed? The organizing industry reports that the average person spends 150 hours a year looking for missing or misplaced items. That's equal to almost one entire month of working time. What could you accomplish if you had that extra month's bonus of time?

Time is your most precious asset. It is the only non-renewable resource. You can plant more trees, generate more energy, earn more money. But you can never have more time than there is. You cannot "save" time nor "spend" it, though we talk as if both were everyday options. Each moment of your life is one slice of eternity that you will never taste again.

So here's the idea. The time you "spend" getting free of clutter can "save" you enough time later to make it a worthwhile "investment" and not an "expense" at all. Is it any wonder we use the language of money to describe our relationship to the treasure of time?

MY GOAL WAS TO COLLECT THE $200

John reports:

> "I'm an old fan of board games. So I pictured my clutter-free campaign as if the whole thing were a board game called TimeQuest. It had squares around the outside of the board. Each square was a task or organizing technique I would commit to doing, right then, for two hours. I used two playing pieces and played against (or with) myself. My first playing piece was a locomotive, because I committed to keeping the campaign moving and on track. The second piece was a tortoise, because I also committed to being slow enough to be thorough.

LOVE IT OR LOSE IT

"Each time I tossed the dice, I wasn't sure where I would land. This felt a lot like my typical day with too much to focus on. Many of the squares held some form of temptation to acquire or keep property I might find in my cleanup campaign. But I had to remember that the goal of my personal campaign was to get around the board and pass GO as often as possible to collect my imaginary $200, which represented two hours of guilt-free time at the gym.

"Occasionally, I would land on a square that had me draw a 'chance' card from the middle of the board. Those cards sometimes gave me a bonus. They said things like, 'Congratulations, your clutter-free desk saves you twenty minutes a day, two hours a week, and a hundred hours a year that you don't spend looking for things.'

"My locomotive kept on chugging and picking up these benefits on its campaign journey. My tortoise kept remembering the book title a few years back, 'If You Don't Have Time To Do It Right, When Will You Have Time To Do It Over?'."

OPTION 2. TRACK THE ACTUAL TIME ORGANIZING TAKES.

Here's an option that can be interesting for those who like details — and can be illuminating even for those who do not.

Many people dread starting a clutter-free campaign. Their dread makes them resist starting. Their resistance adds weight to the entire process. So here's a tool for coming to a starting point with some objective (weightless) detachment.

Your goal is to quantify the time it takes you to organize one area. Select a closet, desk, dresser, or cupboard. Have a timer, pen, and notebook nearby.

Set a timer for fifteen minutes. Record your start time. Pause briefly when the timer dings to record briefly what you accomplished in that quarter hour. Then reset the timer and get back to the task.

THE FIRST 45 MINUTES DID NOT FEEL LIKE PROGRESS

Alex reports:

"I picked the hall closet to start on. It's an area I've been planning to sort out for ages. I started the timer and plunged in. At the end of the first fifteen minutes, I didn't even have it all emptied out. I kept finding things that distracted me. Like the silver button for my dad's jacket. I didn't know where to put that. So I finally took a piece of clear tape, and taped the button to the telephone. That would remind me to call later and tell him it's here. In the second time segment, I finished emptying the closet and vacuumed the floor and the shelves. By the third segment, I had wiped down the walls. So the first 45 minutes was just emptying out and cleaning. It felt good to get this far, but it did not feel like much progress.

"I looked at the two bins of winter hats, scarves, and gloves I had wrestled down from the top shelf. Why would anyone need this much variety? Ah, but the gloves did serve truly different purposes—from the waterproof gardening gloves to warm sledding mittens to

leather driving gloves. I brought down a little-used shoe and purse holder from the bedroom closet. It was the kind that hangs from a single hook and has fourteen vinyl pockets six inches deep. I discovered that each pocket could conveniently hold a rolled-up scarf, a pair of gloves, or several headbands. Best of all, each item was easy to see and to get to. 'This is more like it,' I said to myself, and recorded my progress at the end of the fifth time segment.

"Plunging in again, I took out one coat and jacket to send to the cleaners. Another two coats went into the Goodwill box. The remaining coats and jackets went back into the closet. The stuff that had collected on the closet floor went into a 'limbo' area in the garage. This is the area I now empty on the first of every month. Anything in limbo that doesn't get rescued by a family member gets recycled or donated.

"I stopped then for a cup of tea as I finished my log. I was honestly surprised to find that what I had put off for eight months had taken only one hour and 45 minutes to accomplish."

LOVE IT OR LOSE IT

OPTION 3. BREAK PROJECTS INTO BITE-SIZED PIECES

The book *Cheaper by the Dozen* by Frank B. Gilbreth, Jr., features a family with twelve children and an efficiency expert for a father. You might guess that this particular family had an unusual approach to chores for the children. The smallest children dusted the floors, the middle children washed the dishes, and the tallest older children kept the tops of the furniture clean.

Perhaps you haven't thought ahead far enough to have children who are just the right height for each task. What you might remember from this family's example is the power of seeing each project as a series of smaller tasks that can be accomplished by a team.

Sending out an annual holiday letter, for example, can be seen as a rushed nightmare or as a rewarding time to connect with friends and family. Think of the steps involved:

- Review significant events of the year
- Write the letter
- Select the paper and envelopes
- Check your address list for updates and accuracy
- Address the envelopes

- Write personal messages
- Stamp and seal
- Get them into the mail for timely delivery.

If you send out twenty to fifty letters, it's about a six to eight-hour process or more. It's also coming in December, when you may have one or two other things on your mind. Since few people have a clear six-hour opening on their calendar, chances are you already do this project in bite-sized pieces.

Here's another bite-sized story.

I COULD DO THIS ONE SHELF AT A TIME

Beverly reports:

> "We had lived in this house for fifteen years. We both love boating, and we said this house was the ship for the cruise of our lives. But lately, it was feeling more like the anchor. I hated opening the door of any closet or cupboard. I dreaded a trip to the cluttered laundry room. I apologized to any guests who dared to use the hall coat closet.
>
> "One birthday, I was feeling depressed about all this and I realized that I could change. I

could start a campaign to reclaim my beautiful sleek ship, one shelf at a time. I decided to spend three hours a week on the project. I designed my vision and eliminated my excuses. Then I set aside time for action and decided where to start.

"I picked the laundry room. I cleaned, cleared, organized, and made minor repairs to door handles and shelf supports. In only two of my weekly sessions, I had transformed a place that depressed me to one where all shelves were stable and all supplies were conveniently available.

"I kept going through the hall closet, the linen closet, the bookshelves in the family room, and finally even into my own closet. I was often tempted to quit, but that small commitment of three hours a week brought such good results that I stuck to my resolve. I'm not finished yet, and I know that even when I finish this first cycle, I will need to go back regularly to these same areas. But the ship is once again afloat and that heavy anchor no longer drags me down."

OPTION 4. SCHEDULE A MARATHON MANIA

The best part about this option is that it has a clear starting and ending point—and can get as messy as it needs to in the middle. A true organizing marathon often includes the following:

- A large block of time
- No distractions (banish telephone, computer, non-participating family members and pets for 24-48 hours)
- Basic food and snacks available for breaks
- Six containers (or marked areas) clearly labeled for
  1. Trash
  2. Recycling
  3. Donations
  4. Yard sale
  5. Undecided
  6. Keep (put away later).

Beverly from the last story returns to tell us about her marathon:

IT FELT GOOD TO MAKE A ROYAL MESS AND CLEAN IT ALL UP

She reports:

"That whole process of bite-sized pieces worked everywhere in the house except the kitchen. I knew this was a job that would be best done all at once. I invited my husband to be a partner in this marathon, because I knew he would keep us on target. We started on Saturday morning of a three-day weekend. We figured we could work two days and still have a day to play.

"First, we emptied everything out of the pantry. We had stuff all over the countertops and all across the dining room table. There were even a couple of items neither of us could remember buying or wanting. We washed down all the pantry shelves and arranged things in logical categories according to how we each like to cook. There were some things easy to throw away, like old crackers. Some other items we put into a box for the garage. If we didn't use them in thirty days, we would throw them out. The only possible yard sale item was a three-foot tall pepper mill that we rarely use.

Living Clutter-Free Forever

"Then we emptied all the shelves that held dishes and serving pieces. We cleaned the shelves and tried to cut down on some of our assortment of items. Several sets of glasses were attractive, but we didn't need them. We boxed them to donate. There were an embarrassing number of cleaned cottage cheese containers. We put them into recycling.

"And on it went. We cleaned the spice rack, the oven, and the refrigerator. We sent out for Chinese food, and ate off paper plates. We took a walk just before sunset to clear our heads. We worked till 11 PM and then agreed we needed sleep.

"Up again the next morning, we put on a pot of coffee and cleaned out under the sink as the coffee brewed. We washed the outside of the cabinets and oiled them. Then Tom mopped and waxed the floor while I sat in the dining room and polished the few pieces of silver that we actually use.

"We finished about 11:30 Saturday morning and took ourselves out to lunch. Maybe we were celebrating, or maybe we were too attached to this new pristine kitchen to get it dirty

LOVE IT OR LOSE IT

again so fast. I'm glad I don't spend every weekend like this, but it sure feels good to go in and make a royal mess, and get everything better-than-new in two days."

OPTION 5. HIRE A PROFESSIONAL

Who is a professional? By some definitions, it's anyone who gets paid for their talents and skills. You might prefer someone who is recognized by their peers or recommended by someone you know.

The National Association of Professional Organizers was founded in 1985 to provide professional development and support for consultants who focus on helping clients create their own ideal version of being organized.

Today you can find professional consultants who work on homes or offices and who can help you organize:
• Your technology
• Your children's rooms
• Your closets
• Your photos and mementos
• Your kitchen/garage/attic.

These professionals can bring you three benefits:
• They know how to do the task efficiently and

effectively. They come to each assignment with total focus and no emotional baggage.

- They are here to get it done, not to agonize over how it got so bad in the first place.
- Once you commit the time and budget to work with a professional, you also commit yourself more fully to success.

There are a few questions you want to ask any professional organizer before you select someone to work with:

- What is your schedule and rate for a project like this?
- What references can I contact?
- How will you approach this project?
- How do you make sure it matches my needs and not some abstract definition of "organized?"
- How much will I be involved along the way?
- What supplies or budget will be required (for containers, folders, etc)?
- What is your not-to-exceed estimate of budget and completion date?
- When can you start?

LOVE IT OR LOSE IT

LAUGHTER OPENED ME TO LETTING GO OF THINGS

Maggie reports:

"It was an odd, yet tempting offer. My friend, a professional organizer, called me that morning to ask, 'Hey, Maggie, how'd you like to be featured in a national magazine in a big full-color article?'

"'Tell me more, Gloria. What do I have to do?'

"'Well, the magazine wants to do a 'before and after' article on my organizing company and they wanted to photograph an office that could change from an absolute disaster to a good working environment. I thought yours would be perfect.'

"In exchange for my public embarrassment on a national level, she offered to use her expertise to transform my current clutter into harmony and order. How could I resist?

"The photographer arrived on Tuesday and easily captured the mess on film. He was due back one week later.

"Gloria worked with me for about six hours on Wednesday. The work was hard, satisfying, and surprisingly simple. I learned some basic processes and strategies.

"One exercise had us both sitting on the floor facing each other with a pile of USO's (Unidentified Stacked-up Objects) between us and a trashcan beside us. Gloria lifted one item at a time from the stack. My first job was to say 'trash' or 'save.' That part was easy. The trash claimed page after page. If I voted to save the item, her next line was the stumper. 'And you're saving this because…'

"We got through about ten items. By the third time I heard myself say, 'because it might come in handy some day…' I started smiling. By the fifth time, I laughed at myself. The next time I used that line we both got giddy and fell over onto the floor laughing. I think the laughter was one of the tools that opened me to letting go of so many things.

"After those few valuable hours with the professional at organizing, I had picked up some skills and a rhythm that helped me work alone the next two days. I was ready when the

LOVE IT OR LOSE IT

photographer came back. He was impressed that he didn't need to use special camera angles to fake the improvements. They were real.

"The article appeared a few months later. My friend got publicity and business. I had learned some lifetime skills.

"It's not about clutter; it's about clarity.
It's not about confusion; it's about completion.
It's not about chores; it's about choices
I stand at a new moment in my life."

OPTION 6. EXCHANGE SERVICES

Maybe you make the best eggplant Parmesan on the West Coast, or you take animal portraits that belong in an art gallery, or you are a whiz with tax forms. It is likely you have a gift or skill that others admire. Something you do joyfully and well. It's your unique ability.

It is also likely that you have one or two friends or colleagues who seem very organized. What if you traded services? He helps you organize your computer files and you take a portrait of his puppy. You may look around and find that there are several friends whose talents you can tap. The secret to great results is to be sure you are both trading from generosity — something you are each happy to give. And be sure that you both communicate your expectations clearly.

And sometimes, it doesn't work quite like that. Here's a story that seems slightly off track, but isn't at all. There is no rule that says the trading has to take place within a certain amount of time. The naturally-occurring version of this option is called "reciprocity."

THE CLOSET CLUTTER MATCHED
THE TURMOIL IN MY HEART

Anne reports:

> *"My oldest sister was on her deathbed and I was 3,000 miles away packing to go to her side. My younger sister came by so we could coordinate travel schedules. The minute she said, 'Is there anything I can do to help you?' I lost it.*

> *"We were standing next to my bedroom closet and I burst into blubbering sobs. 'It's this damn closet,' I cursed. 'I can't find the things I need for the trip. Del stayed very calm and walked right into the closet and started neatly folding a*

week's worth of clean laundry still bunched up
exactly as it had come from the dryer two days
ago.

"I know my emotions were about losing my
sister and not about the clutter in the closet.
But in a world where everything seemed sud-
denly unmanageable, the clutter was such a
concrete symbol for the turmoil in my heart.
And so my younger sister and I stood for a few
moments folding laundry. And the underwear
and socks I had been looking for appeared like
magic. This is the 'little sister' I had helped get
her first job and coached through all her col-
lege essays. Today we folded laundry, a
blessed and belated return I never expected. I
don't think anyone else could have helped me
quite so much on that particular day.

"For, as we touched the familiar socks, sheets,
and towels, the world came back into a familiar
pattern. And maybe that's the way each of us
gets through upheaval. One day at a time, one
kindness at a time, one pile of folded laundry at
a time."

Living Clutter-Free Forever

STEP FOUR – SELECT YOUR TOOLS

*Have nothing in your houses that you do not know to be useful
or believe to be beautiful.*
William Morris

What You Love, You Preserve

Approaching this step, remember that what you love, you use, and you preserve. And what doesn't work for you personally will never be a valuable support, no matter how many other people rave about it.

Options for taking the fourth step:

- Select what you need every day
- Contain those items efficiently and aesthetically
- Arrange elements in a system that works for you
- Support your system with technology
- Find tools you enjoy using
- Let go of anything that fails the three-question test.

SHE WASN'T REALLY ALLERGIC TO CALENDARS

What you love, you use and preserve. One of our favorite clients was convinced she hated calendars. "I must be allergic to them," she complained. "I've never found a calendar I could follow. I lose them. I forget to look at them. They just won't ever work for me." She also reported that she sometimes missed meetings or showed up late, "Because I didn't have it on my calendar."

We interviewed her about her taste in art, the size of her purse, her favorite colors, and other seemingly unrelated elements. Then we took a rewarding tour of bookstores, stationery stores, and office supply warehouses. We selected three calendars that might work and wrapped them in a gift box. She opened the box and fell in love with a red leather 4 x 6 notebook that had a botanical print on the front and several inside pockets to hold notecards and pictures.

Suddenly, a calendar was no longer a nagging reminder of things left undone. It was a pleasant companion that also held family and vacation photos.

There is, of course, no magic system or product that is right for every home or office. Devise a system you can love and you'll reduce clutter enormously. This

Living Clutter-Free Forever

magic comes not because you have increased the efficiency of the system, but because you have decreased your resistance to preserving, protecting, and maintaining it. You have made yourself an offer you don't want to refuse!

OPTIONS FOR SELECTING YOUR TOOLS

OPTION 1. KEEP CLOSEST WHAT YOU USE MOST OFTEN

Sit at your desk with your eyes closed. Now think of the work you do most often at this location. Can you reach across your desk or into an easily accessible drawer and touch the items you need to complete that work? Can you touch the directory that you use to research addresses three to five times a day? Can you touch the stapler you need for attaching receipts before you forward documents? Can you reach the paper stock you use almost every day to refill your printer?

If these are things you use every day, they should be within arm's reach and not smothered by piles of stuff on top of them.

LOVE IT OR LOSE IT

Most of us do reasonably well at this in the work setting. Now imagine yourself in other settings in your life. Can you pass the same test as you stand in your kitchen, or in front of your medicine cabinet, or in your closet? Or is your bottle of vitamin C hiding behind all those cold remedies you've been using on the kids this week? And on Tuesday, you forgot to take the vitamin C and on Wednesday, you forgot again. And on Thursday you started sniffling.

Lot tho law of proximity help you. Keep closest what you use most often.

Invest wisely in things you touch most often. Have the best stapler you can find if you use it often. Don't let yourself be frustrated by a tape dispenser that twists the tape. Get full-spectrum lighting for your work area. Put your pampering budget into these daily tools and you will feel the rewards every day.

I BOUGHT THREE
AND PUT THEM IN ARM'S REACH

Kathy reports:

> *"I'm generally a frugal person, yet I make it a point to indulge myself on the things I touch every day. I'm clear about my priorities. I don't*

just buy a hairbrush because it's on sale at the drug store. I talk to three friends and a hairdresser and select exactly the right one for my hair. I don't just buy the sheets with a stylish print. I check thread count and stitching. Once I spent almost three weeks selecting a perfect pen. I tested several models for their weight, balance, and ink flow. When I found just the right one, I bought three of them and put each within arm's reach of the three primary places I need a pen.

"You'd think I'd be analytical about every part of life, but I'm not. I'll read about a special airfare in the Sunday travel section of the newspaper and spontaneously schedule a family trip to Vermont. I hope to take a lot of week-long vacations, but I'll probably be using my hairbrush and these pens for the next twenty years.

"I'm also a nut about scissors. I grew up in a household with one pair of scissors that resided in my mother's sewing basket, and was always returned there immediately after using. I was startled once when a friend gave me a pair of scissors for my kitchen. 'But I already own scissors,' I protested. She laughed at me

LOVE IT OR LOSE IT

and said 'You can have more than one pair.'
What an idea! I put one pair in my kitchen, one
in the office, the bedroom, and the laundry. I
felt so rich."

OPTION 2. CONTAIN NEEDED ITEMS EFFICIENTLY AND AESTHETICALLY

Here's where logic and creativity can intersect. Your goal in containing the items you need is to have them conveniently available when and where you need them. This may involve the use of a utilitarian filing cabinet, great at holding quantities of documents in visible and upright display. It may also involve a stuffed teddy bear sitting on the corner of your desk to hold your reading glasses. If you always put your glasses on the bear, and you can easily find and reach them, then that bear may be your ideal container.

IT HELPS TO REMIND ME
THAT THE OFFICE IS CLOSED

Annie's story:

"My home office is a sun-drenched loft off the
master bedroom. I love it, and I had two big
challenges in making it efficient. First, I hated

the idea of filing cabinets in such an open space, but I needed someplace to store basic documents. Second, the loft has no doors, and therefore no door to shut when I want to feel like the office is closed.

"When I looked at all the elements carefully, I realized I could tuck an upright filing cabinet neatly inside my bedroom closet—for archives and files I rarely needed to get to. It might also help me reign in my impulse to stuff more clothes in there.

"Then I had to figure out how to give myself the feeling of doors to close. I usually work with at least four or five active files scattered around me. I laugh at this pattern sometimes and assume I'm trying to do multi-tasking in my subconscious. Anyway, I do try to put all those files away at the end of each day. I just didn't have a clear and consistent version of what 'putting them away' meant.

"Sometimes I'd stack them under the tele-phone, sometimes next to the computer, some-times in an antique washtub that serves as my perpetual inbox.

LOVE IT OR LOSE IT

"Finally I cleared off a shelf in the bookcase next to my computer area. I went to one of the stores that specializes in everything you need for getting organized. I selected three containers that would match my bookcase and hold my file folders efficiently.

"I came home and sorted the items in my working office. Some went in the first bin—files I am actively working on this week. Some went in the second—files on projects for the next six months. And some went in bin three—file index, calendar, tickler file, and basic stationery and forms. Most mornings I 'open' the office by placing bins one and three on top of the two-shelf bookcase. The files are easily available, and not spread out. Best of all, when I want to feel finished for the day, I pack up the bins, put them back on the shelf, and turn off the lights for the night.

"I have to admit that I still feel pulled to step back into the office more than I'd prefer. But I find that this system helps me remind myself that there are times when the office is 'closed'."

OPTION 3. ARRANGE ELEMENTS IN A SYSTEM THAT WORKS FOR YOU

Do you alphabetize your spices, color-code your closets, and keep all your telephone messages in a continuous running written log? If so, you have a system. The only question is, does that system work for you? Here are three ways to check that out:

- You like the system
- It does what you need it to do
- It is reasonable to maintain.

You probably have a whole series of invisible systems in your life already. You have a system for sorting the laundry, one for filling the dishwasher, one for keeping track of important phone calls.

It's great if your system looks good to others, but it is essential that it helps you operate more smoothly in your everyday life. Your systems probably evolved over time. Maybe you used to have a paper and pen by your telephone. This was about all you needed for taking down information. Then someone invented 'Hold.' Now you needed extra supplies by the telephone to keep yourself occupied while waiting for a human voice to respond. So you got a shoulder caddy for your telephone and added that to your telephone 'system.' At some point you may switch to a headset telephone or a speaker phone, so you can fill the time while on "hold."

This is a good time to take a look at some of your systems. Notice how they have evolved in response to changing circumstances or technology, and evaluate whether they are still meeting your needs.

SOME THINGS ARE MORE IMPORTANT THAN EFFICIENCY

Chuck reports:

> "Everybody smiles at the old story of the woman who always cut three inches off the end of a roast before she cooked it, and saved that small section to cook later. One day, her husband asked her why she did that. She responded that she did it because her mother always did it. At Thanksgiving, they asked her mother about the practice, and her mother reported that she did it because she had watched her own mother do the same thing. They cornered grandma, who laughed and said she did it because her roaster was too small to hold the whole roast. That story reminds me that we are always learning systems

from the people we care about, but not always what we think at first they are teaching.

"Well, when I was a kid, my dad had one of those hand-held utility lights with the wire cage around the bulb and a hook on the end. One of my most vivid childhood memories is helping him fix the car. My job was always to hold the light. Dad always told me where to point the light, and it seemed like I could never keep it on the target area. If I was supposed to keep it on the spark plugs, I'd let it wander back to his hands, or somewhere else in the engine. I always said it was because my arms were so tired, but I guess I just couldn't pay attention for that long.

"It was years later before it dawned on me that my dad didn't necessarily need me to hold the light, and that it wasn't entirely about whether I did the job well. He wanted me to smell the oil and the grease of the engine, and get the sense of working on a car and being mechanically self-sufficient. When I grew up and had cars and finally even a garage, the first thing I bought was one of those utility lights with a hook.

LOVE IT OR LOSE IT

"For Christmas that year, my wife surprised me with a light on an adjustable strap that fits around my head. I can direct the light exactly where I want it with just a twist of my head. For most jobs, it's actually a much better tool than the light with a hook. But I put the old-fashioned light safely away for one specific purpose. When my daughter gets a little older, and she wants to help me in the garage, I'll get out the light with the hook and go back to the old system. Some things are more important than efficiency."

OPTION 4. SUPPORT YOUR SYSTEM WITH TECHNOLOGY

Most people today assume that technology means computers or gadgets. But technology has always been around to support or sabotage human endeavor. One client remembered the best technology she'd ever observed. Her Uncle Conn used wonderfully simple "technology" to keep track of the tools in his basement workshop. He had a giant pegboard mounted to the wall. He painted it white. He then placed each tool on the pegboard, outlined it, and painted in the outline in the shape of the tool.

What a great system! It was clear. It was simple. Anyone could follow the plan. Uncle Conn could see from across the room whether an item he needed was there or not. Best of all, it never needed upgrading or crashed or destroyed his data.

Of course, you want to select the technology that is the perfect blend of price, function, and benefits. You want the best you can afford, that is also reliable, and matches your technical sophistication and needs. Even more importantly, it has to be something you will use. If it does not prove valuable over time, you need to get rid of it.

IT LURKS ON MY SHELF, TAUNTING ME

Kerry reports:

> *"I fell in love with that TV commercial that shows a person sitting near the ocean dictating into a recorder that later types up her words on her computer. I had just started on a new project that involved taking handwritten records and entering them into the computer. 'This is the perfect time for me to buy some voice recognition software,' I thought. I pictured myself dictating, while taking long morning*

LOVE IT OR LOSE IT

walks and letting the computer transcribe my words magically while I was in the shower.

"I bought the top-of-the-line software package that even included the custom tape recorder that hooked up to the computer for downloading data. I was patient. I expected to invest a good twelve to twenty hours in learning to use this program. I upgraded my computer memory, worked through the tutorial twice, trained the software to recognize my voice patterns, and set aside additional blocks of time to experiment and learn to use the software smoothly. But every time I would dictate, something would go wrong. I checked with a friend, but he had a different brand of software that worked pretty well for him.

"I know I'm not really into technology, but I felt like I gave this a solid try. I just never could get it to work for me. So now it lurks there on my shelf, taunting me for my wastefulness and inefficiency. I guess it's time to donate it to my neighborhood elementary school where the kids will probably master it in a minute. I finally came back to the technology that works best for me. I plunk my bottom on a chair and work at my computer till it's done!"

Living Clutter-Free Forever

OPTION 5. FIND TOOLS YOU ENJOY USING

One toddler's favorite tool is an art-crafted rattle and teething ring. She can make noise and bite into something soft at the same time.

Author Thomas Wolfe helped his mother operate a boarding house in Asheville, North Carolina. The paying boarders were given all the best places in the house, so Wolfe had very little space to call his own. Late at night, when he could finally find some privacy in the kitchen, the tall aspiring author hand-wrote his stories using the top of the refrigerator for his desk.

Both the toddler and the novelist found the tools that were right for them. You can too. They will be the tools that suit you personally and that you enjoy using.

I INVENTED THE GAME OF "ONE HUNDRED TREASURES"

Julie tells her story:

> "I invented a game for myself a while ago. I call it 'One Hundred Treasures.' I start the game by thinking I am somewhere like a beach condo. This place has all the absolute basics—rental furniture, appliances, kitchenware, and linens.

LOVE IT OR LOSE IT

*Beyond those basics, what one hundred trea-
sures would I choose to have around me if I
needed to stay there six months or more?*

*"I lumped all essential toiletries into one item
(toothpaste, toothbrush, soap, shampoo, etc.). I
lumped essential underwear and socks into
one item. A third 'lump' item included essential
first aid and safety supplies. Beyond that,
everything I selected counted on my list.*

*"I knew immediately that I couldn't just use the
basic cookware. I selected my mom's enamel
roaster and my special pasta pot. I decided I
could do without bedroom furniture upgrades,
but I wanted our family room couch and coffee
table. I didn't need half the makeup supplies I
store at home, but I did select my Waterford
crystal blush brush because each of my sisters
and my daughter-in-law has one, and we often
think of each other when we use them.*

*"Shoes were a wonderful indulgence. Just
think, I could get two of something to count as
one single item! I used up nine of my hundred
items on shoes.*

"So what did I learn from doing this exercise? I learned that there are some of my tools for living that I am exceedingly attached to. I don't especially care if the attachment is based on feelings, function, beauty, habit, or comfort. The exercise helped me rediscover how fond I am of many items in my life.

"I also realized how much of the stuff around me doesn't add much to my comfort, efficiency, or joy. I remember a principle of design that says, 'Anything that does not add, subtracts.' I usually view all this extra stuff as neither positive nor negative. It's just neutral. It's just there. But that can't be true. If it doesn't add anything, and it takes up space in my life, it is already a negative.

"This exercise is one more window through which I see the pattern of clutter in my life's landscape. As I clarify my attachment to the things I enjoy using, I find I have no need for the things that are merely clutter."

OPTION 6. LET GO OF ANYTHING THAT FAILS THE THREE-QUESTION TEST

Remember again the three-question test for any item in your life:

- Is it useful?
- Is it beautiful?
- Do you love it?

Unless an item meets one of those standards, get rid of it. If it meets two of them, take good care of it. If it meets all three, treasure it, and appreciate it as a gift of good fortune.

The ceramic ashtray your son made in nursery school may fail the first two, but pass the third. Your lawn mower may fail tests two and three, but it's hard to mow your lawn with a beautiful painting.

Give yourself a challenge right this moment. If you are at home, at work, or anyplace where you have direct influence over the setting, test ten things near you with these three questions.

Keep the three questions in your head and continue asking them until everything around you fits into one of those categories. Some items will puzzle you. One item may be useful, but it needs some repair. Then fix it. It is not useful in its current state. One item may be beautiful, but just doesn't go with anything else in your house. Then give it away. Or maybe there is something you love, but it is more perfect for someone else in your family. Then let it go, while keeping visitation rights.

ONCE IT WAS THERE, THERE IT WAS

Mark reports:

"I don't know how all this stuff got into my life. But once it was there, there it was. And I rarely found reason to get rid of anything.

"I'm too thrifty to throw away anything that's perfectly good. So I never asked myself, 'good for what or good for whom?'
Here are just a few of the items these questions helped me let go of:

*   *A complete set of snowtires for a truck we sold two years ago*
*   *Twenty-five years of National Geographic magazines*
*   *The nametags I've collected from every conference I've attended in the last fifteen years*

- *Halloween costumes for our kids who have now gone off to college*
- *An ugly lamp we never liked*
- *A stuffed owl we inherited when some neighbors moved.*

"The list goes on. Now I challenge myself to find and get rid of one item each day that fails the three-question test. At this rate, I may be clutter-free in about a hundred years. But that's not the point. I am keeping myself more aware that holding on to clutter is a daily decision. And I can make better decisions."

STEP FIVE - MAINTAIN YOUR SUCCESS

To want in one's heart to do a thing for its own sake; to enjoy doing it; to concentrate all one's energies upon it — that's not only the surest guarantee of success. It is also being true to oneself.
Amelia Earhart

Live Clutter-Free Forever
Approaching this step, know that you are well on your way to living clutter-free forever!

Options for taking the fifth step:
- Revisit the freedom of your clutter-free, ideal setting
- Explore holding on and letting go
- Identify other users who will benefit from your surplus
- Schedule a time and select a plan for regular attention to organizing
- Create systems of support and/or accountability
- Celebrate successes

CUTTER-FREE LIVING AS A CHOICE, NOT A CHORE

So how can you live clutter-free forever? Let's presume that you've been working on the first four steps of the *Love It Or Lose It* process and you've officially resigned from the Stuff-of-the-Month club. You are already tasting some of the joys and freedom of letting go of clutter. This is the time to look at preserving and maintaining the progress you are making. This is the time to permanently embrace clutter-free living as a choice — not a chore.

The best way to do this is to review everything that has worked for you so far and to insert those actions into your everyday life. This is the time to recycle your success and keep the process flowing.

OPTIONS FOR MAINTAINING YOUR SUCCESS

OPTION 1. REVISIT THE FREEDOM OF YOUR CLUTTER-FREE IDEAL SETTING

Think back to your vision of your ideal setting, your ideal desk, and maybe your ideal linen closet. How has that vision emerged or evolved since you started this whole campaign? Write down a few words that describe what you wanted to experience in that setting:

Harmony　　　　　*Flow*
Comfort　　　　　*Efficiency*
Open space　　　*Relaxation*
Focus　　　　　　*No distractions*
Pleasure　　　　*Peace of mind*
Everything at my fingertips
Everything working smoothly

Overall, it's an environment where I feel invited, perhaps even called, to do my best.

Revisit and revise your version of an ideal setting. Do this regularly, and your vision can act as a magnet, attracting you toward what you want from this point forward. For many people, this is much more powerful than merely avoiding what you don't want.

THEIR COLOR AND FRAGRANCE
FLOWED EVERYWHERE

Carol reports:

"As I worked through the steps, I learned something surprising about myself. I already knew that guilt and obligation are not strong

LOVE IT OR LOSE IT

motivators for me. Whenever anyone suggests that I should take an action because it is my duty or responsibility, I resist like crazy. I guess I still have a lot of rebellious teenager in me somewhere. I could probably go through counseling to tame that rebellious undercurrent, but this process showed me a more pleasing and satisfying path.

"Since guilt and obligation do not work for me, I wondered, what does work? When do I, with natural ease and joy, plunge into a task and operate at my best?

"One day, I stopped on the way home from work to pick up flowers. I was hosting a dinner party the next night, and figured I'd get one more chore out of the way. The florist had a special on deep-red roses, so that's what I selected. As soon as I got home, I trimmed the flowers and arranged them with greenery. Too tall for a table centerpiece, the flowers graced the entry table perfectly. The instant I placed the flowers in the entry area, their color and fragrance flowed into the adjoining rooms.

"Now I wanted the whole area to be a home for that bouquet. As I worked on cleaning and *arranging the dining room, I kept glancing over to enjoy the splendor of those roses. I even wished the vacuum were quieter, so as not to disturb their silent beauty.*

"So now I sometimes pick a starting point of simple beauty, and let that central point inspire me as I work through a room. It may be flowers; it may be a rearranged selection of photographs on the mantelpiece. Once, it was even a new coffeemaker (beauty can come in many forms).

"The important thing for me to recognize is that I operate best from inspiration, and not from obligation."

OPTION 2. EXPLORE HOLDING ON AND LETTING GO

You don't need go too deeply into psychology to know that holding on to things forms some type of security blanket around you.

- We hold on to photos, music, videos and mementos to preserve memories.
- We hold on to clothing to preserve the touch or smell of someone we love.

- We hold on to fifteen-year-old pay stubs because throwing them away eliminates a piece of our past.
- We hold on to tax forms and legal documents, for fear that we will be told to produce them some day.

We also hold onto things because of significant emotional events in our lives.

- Some people who remember the Depression still save every plastic bag they ever encounter, and have a hard time throwing anything away.
- People who have had a significant loss sometimes exercise their power to hold on to *things*, because they felt powerless to hold on to a *person*, a *job*, or a *home* they lost in the past.

You have your own instinctive response to holding on or letting go. This is a good time to take a look at that reaction. Here are a few questions you might ask yourself:

- What's something I could easily let go of, but just haven't gotten around to yet?
- What's something I could easily let go of, if I knew somebody else could use it?
- What's something I'm not inclined to part with, but would feel good about donating, if I saw a real need?

- What's something I don't use much, but still wouldn't part with except in extreme circumstances?

Begin to identify your own "comfort location" on the continuum of Holding On or Letting Go. On the extreme left of the continuum (1 on a scale of 100) is the feeling, "I need to hold on to everything I can. I'm happiest when holding firm." On the right (100 on the continuum), is the feeling, "Letting go of everything I can liberates me. I'm happiest when feeling free."

What number represents your most automatic and comfortable point on the continuum now? What would you like it to be? What are some things you can do to get from here to there?

IT WAS THE FIRST LUXURY
WE ALLOWED OURSELVES

Barbara reflects on her piano:

> "The piano is far from perfect. It can go out of tune with a whisper of humidity. It also takes up an enormous amount of space. Still, I'm reluctant to let it go. It was the first luxury we allowed ourselves when we were missionaries in India, and before we had the children.

"This piano has been with me through seven-teen moves, even eating up space in a tiny apartment in New York City, when we lived there for two years.

"But now the kids are on their own and I don't play it much anymore. I often feel some sad-ness when I look at the piano. I wondered if I might be ready to let it go, but I was still feeling connected to it. Then one day I did some work with a gifted photographer. A couple of the pictures in his portfolio were of furniture. The photographs looked like 'portraits' of the furni-ture, somehow capturing personality as well as surfaces.

"I have asked him to do a portrait of my piano with soft light slipping in the window and a tray of fresh African violets next to the candles beside the sheet music. The piano will look like it's inviting me to sit down and play. I can have him print the photograph on canvas paper, surround the image with a beautiful frame, and keep my piano with me forever.

"And the real piano can be auctioned off for a fund-raiser for the women and children's shel-ter. It is satisfying to know that I can still love

something, while letting it move on to another place where it will be valued."

WHEN OVERRESPONSIBILITY BECOMES IRRESPONSIBILITY

Here's Flo's story:

"When I first became an organizing consultant, I worked with one client who helped me learn an important lesson I've used ever since. This woman was in her 60's, still vital and active in her work, but approaching retirement. She saw her role in life as 'the keeper of the flame.' She liked being the family beacon — the one everybody would turn to in times of need.

"She had an attic stuffed with furniture and clothes, all in great condition. If one of the nephews needed a table for his first apartment, he could visit Molly's attic. If one of her children needed a 1960's outfit for a Halloween costume or a community theatre production, Molly's attic was always open. If her grandson needed a rotary telephone for a show-and-tell history speech in school, Molly's attic could provide. Molly's attic was a family institution.

LOVE IT OR LOSE IT

"When Molly looked at retirement, she resolved to sort out everything in her attic. She brought me in to help her get the attic organized. By the end of our first session, I could easily tell that she didn't really want to organize her attic. She wanted to move on with her life.

"I probed gently about her retirement plans, and learned that she and her husband wanted to move to a smaller place and feel more free to travel, but she was afraid that her family needed her to keep operating the big house and attic so familiar to them all. As she had done for so much of her life, Molly was willing to let her own dreams be denied to meet family expectations. She was letting overresponsibility toward others become irresponsibility toward herself.

"I suggested she talk to her children about the possibility of her moving. She did. Two out of the three were ninety-percent fine with the idea. Even the reluctant son came around, once the shock of impending change wore off.

"I worked with Molly several times in the months before her move. We found just the right place to sell or donate almost everything

from Molly's attic. And family members claimed treasures they could then be responsible for themselves. She was especially pleased that most of her work wardrobe went to a program for women reentering the workforce. Her clothes could help another mother find a job and raise a family.

"I talked to her again a few months later. 'I loved operating Molly's attic all those years, and now I'm glad to let it go. It was time for a new role in my life'."

OPTION 3. IDENTIFY OTHERS WHO WILL BENEFIT FROM YOUR SURPLUS

Many clients find it easier to get rid of clutter when they donate their surplus to a charity, or to an educational cause. They like thinking of others who will benefit from what they no longer need. Most people immediately think of Goodwill Industries and other organizations they have known about for a long time And yet you can also add a spark of creativity to finding the right place to make a recycling donation.

One client told of finding big manila envelopes stuffed with Christmas cards she had received over the years. She always imagined that some day she would

LOVE IT OR LOSE IT

find the time to go back and enjoy them, perhaps reminiscing over notes from friends and photos she had forgotten about.

A friend told her about St Jude's Ranch for Children in Boulder City, Nevada. They accept donations of the fronts of any greeting cards. They recycle these card fronts into new cards as a fundraising program. "Since St Jude is the patron saint of hopeless causes," the friend remarked, "maybe he'd be the perfect inspiration for your clutter-free campaign."

Here are several more recycling stories.

THEY COULD EASILY POSE A FIRE HAZARD

Barbara reports:

> "My husband loves magazines, and we subscribe to nineteen of them. Fortunately, most of them only come once a month. Even so, they could easily pose a fire hazard if we just stacked them up and waited for time to read them all. My cousin, Judy, stops by early every Monday morning. We share a brief visit and she collects our latest magazines for the waiting room of the dental practice where she works. Her schedule of coming

by every Monday for the latest issues serves three good purposes:

- *We read or get rid of the magazines quickly.*
- *Judy reports that her patients often praise her wide selection of current titles.*
- *I see my cousin regularly."*

WE DONATED THE STORY DOLL

Rita reports:

"My great-niece, Liz, was born premature with spinal complications, and needed fifteen surgeries on her legs before she was ten years old. I thought she might be intrigued to study more about the body in general, and all the parts of herself that were working so well. So I bought an anatomical doll from a medical catalog.

"The large doll had Velcro strips down her torso, and opened up to reveal layers of internal organs. The doll had been designed by a dad who wanted to help his own child and her siblings understand the medical procedures the child was having. He later produced more copies to help parents and doctors talk with children about their bodies.

LOVE IT OR LOSE IT

"My great-niece appreciated the thought, but the doll turned out to be more of a teaching tool than a toy. So I stored it away on an upper shelf in my closet, hoping no other kids I knew would ever need it.

"One day, a friend mentioned that the Ronald McDonald House was looking for donations. They needed anything that would help family members housed there temporarily while visiting their hospitalized children. Why didn't I think of this before? It was the perfect place for the doll.

"Liz thought donating the doll was a great idea. We dressed the doll in a new hospital gown with bright blue stripes and off she went to help other children."

OPTION 4. SCHEDULE TIME FOR ORGANIZING

Maybe you clean off your desk and check tomorrow's calendar before you leave work each day. Maybe you get the table cleared, and the kitchen cleaned up after each meal. Maybe you check your smoke detector batteries twice a year, as you reset your clocks for the start and finish of Daylight Savings Time. If so, you already do schedule some time regularly for

Living Clutter-Free Forever

organizing. Now you might look at expanding those patterns. Here's a question few of us have ever asked ourselves:

What amount of time would it take each day, week, month, or quarter to keep my home or work setting in ideal (not necessarily perfect) condition?

And here's a challenge:
For the next four to six weeks, schedule that amount of time and use the time you schedule. At the end of this experiment, notice the changes you see in your life and work. If the results are worth it, continue investing the time.

And remember, you don't need to do all this by yourself. You can delegate or hire help for some of the tasks.

WE GO TO THE RAINY-DAY JAR

Sibyl had an interesting variation on setting time aside:

> *"We both work hard. When weekends come, we like to relax, but there's so much to do. With grocery shopping, laundry, errands, and car*

LOVE IT OR LOSE IT

maintenance to think about, we tend to let the clutter gradually accumulate. It's just too easy to let things slide.

"This year we resolved to commit a minimum of three hours a month to special projects attacking clutter. We work together on these projects to avoid the detour of setting aside things that may be important to the other person. The first of every month, we decide on a block of time, we schedule it on our calendars, and choose together what project we can tackle in that amount of time. We sometimes work on a Saturday morning, and sometimes plunge in on a Thursday or Friday after work and a quick dinner.

"Some projects, like painting the guest room, take longer than three hours. But our rhythm of doing one project a month helps us see that after we get that much done, the rest doesn't seem quite so daunting. We also discover a lot of small tasks within bigger projects. Maybe a small repair that needs to be done, or a shelf lining that needs replacing, or a ceiling fan that needs a good cleaning. Rather than stop the big project, we make a note of the task. That note joins others in our 'Rainy Day Jar.'

Living Clutter-Free Forever

"The jar collects notes on tasks that will take less than thirty minutes to complete. Anything we notice that we can't tend to right away, we write down and place in the jar. We color code the notes: green, if Roger needs to do it, blue for me, and white for either of us. We each try to do one or two a week. If a rainy day cancels a picnic or outdoor plan, we may spend two hours doing items from the jar. We are allowed to 'cheat' slightly by pulling two or three items, and then choosing one to do immediately. The others go back in the jar.

"And, just to add a little spice, there are always three items in the jar that are treats instead of tasks. Believe me, if I'm set for a chore and draw the note that says, 'Go out for an ice cream cone,' that's the one I pick."

OPTION 5. CREATE A SYSTEM OF SUPPORT OR ACCOUNTABILITY

If you are a totally self-sufficient person, you may not need any help or want anyone to pat you on the back and say, "good work." Although most of us do need some support along the way.

One client commented, "I have a cleaning service come in for about two hours once a month. They do the bathrooms, mirrors, floors, dusting, and vacuuming. I need to get all the surfaces cleared off before they come, so they can do their work. So that's one way I give myself a monthly deadline. After they leave, the place just smells so good, I'm motivated to take on a new project myself. Sometimes I wash the windows or straighten up the hall closet or clean out the refrigerator. I like doing a project like that, every month or so."

Others turn to friends or colleagues to hear someone ask, "What did you accomplish?" and then the best part, "Good job!"

NO MESS; NO APOLOGIES

Jenny reports:

> "It was odd how we got started. We had a session at work on public speaking, and the topic I chose for my impromptu speech was 'The Love It or Lose It Principle.' After my two-minute presentation, several other people from across the company came up and asked me more about it. Five of us met for lunch the

following Monday, and I told them more about the five-step Clutter Campaign, confessing that I was only starting Step Two.

"They all wanted to join in and launch their own campaigns. Dan suggested it might be easier to keep with the process if we met regularly to share our struggles and successes. We all agreed to meet for lunch every second Monday. Our goal before the first session was to complete Step One, Option One, 'Assess what your setting is like right now.'

"We had a very spirited session on that topic. We seemed to be playing 'can-you-top-this' about how bad our settings were at that point. By the next session, we had already lost one guy who said he was just too busy to take time to get organized right now. The rest of us continued working through the options at the rate of one every two weeks. When a suggested option didn't quite suit our needs, we could pass — or come up with our own variation.

"One creative wrinkle was that Cathy's ten-year-old daughter, Kelly, came to work with her one day for Take-Your-Daughter-To-Work Day.

Kelly was playing with a microcassette recorder when her mom started to look for something. Kelly did about a three-minute play-by-play coverage of the fruitless search, and even captured her mother's frustrated comment at the end, when she still couldn't find the folder. Cathy played the tape for us, and told us that she would hold on to that tape to help her track her progress in her clutter-free campaign.

"This is not a fast process. But just knowing I have a team to report to every two weeks keeps me committed. We all started with a focus on our work settings, but most of us have commented that the patterns are spilling over into our home lives too. And for the first time ever, I never have to apologize to passengers for the mess in my car. No mess; no apologies."

I CAN SEE MORE CLEARLY
WHAT TO HOLD ON TO

Maura reports:

"I first met some of my friends when we did 'Mommy and Me' swim sessions at the gym a few years back. We all had very busy lives and were grateful for the luxury of time with our

children and with each other. As the kids got to nursery school age, we sometimes met for coffee and conversation.

"One day, Megan said she had been inspired by a prayer she had read in the newspaper. It was written by the Franciscan friar, Mychal Judge, the New York Fire Department chaplain who was killed by falling debris in the World Trade Center attack in 2001. Here's what he wrote:

> Lord, take me where You want me to go;
> Let me meet who You want me to meet;
> Tell me what You want me to say, and
> Keep me out of Your way.

"This short prayer, so perfectly suited to both his life and his death, inspired Megan to write her own prayer to help keep life in perspective whenever she feel trapped by turmoil.

> Lord, help me know what to let go of,
> so I can see more clearly what to hold on to.

"She invited us to join her in a 'Love It or Lose It' campaign for five months. Each month, we would take one of the steps, do what we could

LOVE IT OR LOSE IT

with it, and report our results when we got together. The reports were fascinating and sometimes funny.

"Kim admitted that she opened a drawer at work and a colleague saw her bin of leftover soy sauce packets from carryout lunch orders. 'Why do you have so many tiny packets of soy sauce in your desk?' he asked.

"'Because I hate it.' she answered. Then she heard herself, laughed, and dumped all the packets in the trash.

"One of the most helpful parts of our sessions was that we saved ten minutes at the end to each say one thing we had learned that day from someone else in the group. This helped remind us that we are all learning resources for each other. And a group of moms with kids of similar ages may offer each other as much wisdom as any other experts on earth.

OPTION 6. CELEBRATE SUCCESSES

Finally, you can breathe free. You have created a setting where everything you are or wish to be is supported by everything around you, and nothing extra weighs you down. Congratulations. It's time to celebrate. Celebrate your tenacity; celebrate your results in reaching your ideal setting. Celebrate the fact you plan to keep it that way.

The form and flavor of your celebration will probably be as individual as you are. One woman was so pleased with her newly organized office that she decided to sleep there on her couch the first night and "wake up to see the morning sunlight shining off clear and gleaming surfaces." Another home office entrepreneur took a whole roll of pictures of his work area exactly the way he likes it. "This is to remind me how good it can be, in case I collapse into clutter again," he said.

The interesting thing about celebrations, though, is that they mark the accomplishment of one thing and the beginning of the next challenge. You celebrate landing a big contract, knowing that the work itself is not yet begun. You celebrate a hole-in-one in golf, knowing that you have now escalated your own expectations of your personal best. You celebrate the birth of a baby, knowing full well that the challenge of being a parent is still in front of you. The celebration is never the end. It's a moment of congratulatory pause before a new beginning.

LOVE IT OR LOSE IT

WE FINISH WITH EMPTIER SPACES
AND FULLER HEARTS

Here's a story of Alice's celebration:

"We are a very active family in a very small house. Sometimes I look back on the last fifteen years as a succession of kids' toys, clothes, sports equipment, and musical instruments. The swimming, hockey, and badminton equipment took over as the girls hit about eight, but the musical instruments had been with us forever. They started with drums and triangles as toddlers, and moved on to guitars, banjos, an accordion, flute, and piano. Thank heaven for rental instruments.

"John and I have similarly wide-ranging interests in computers, photography, crafts, spiritual exploration, and books galore. My business takes me to gift shows several times a year, and I frequently acquire items for friends, or to have on display. We have so much stuff, we give over one treasured parking slot in our basement garage to storing some of it.

"About once a year, I get the fever to clear stuff out. Maybe it's the spring equinox. I've tried

Living Clutter-Free Forever

yard sales, but now I have something I like much better. I hold an open-driveway party. The family and I invite friends and neighbors to come by, socialize, and take home something on display.

"I realized that some people might be offended if they saw anything they had given me on one of the take-home tables. So I state clearly on the invitation:

"'Don't be surprised if some of the items available for selection look familiar. It may even be something you gave me yourself. Please know that your gift was appreciated, used, and enjoyed, and is now ready for another welcoming home.'

"Not only are people not offended, I've had several friends reclaim something they had given me. They make comments like, 'I always liked this cookie jar. It will be perfect in my pantry.'

"The party is much better than a yard sale. We don't have to put price tags on anything. Everybody has fun. And we come away with emptier spaces and fuller hearts."

LOVE IT OR LOSE IT

PART III
WHERE DO I GO FROM HERE?

It's not about the clutter.
It's about what my life could be like without it.
Bridget Cavarocchi

ASK QUESTIONS ALONG THE WAY

Any journey into the unknown is likely to prompt questions. What's important is to accept that fact and keep asking those questions. Here are nine common questions people ask:

Question 1. WHAT'S THE TOUGHEST CLUTTER TRAP TO ESCAPE?

While it's hard to work in a clutter-entrenched business, drowning in a sea of paper that's been flooding up for years, that's not the biggest challenge. The toughest traps are those that hit you when you are most vulnerable — such as right after the death of a family member. This is even more wrenching than our earlier example of moving a parent into assisted living. This time you know it is really over, and you are not as prepared as you thought you would be. There are also thousands of details that must be addressed in a short period of time.

You are spilling over with emotion; you may be torn between grief, anger, relief, and despair. Suddenly, you are expected to deal logically with everything that remains of a person's physical and financial universe. You've lost your sense of proportion and all questions seem to be of equal weight. What do you do with a

LOVE IT OR LOSE IT

half-empty box of Band-Aids? And where was that key to the safe deposit box? Both questions sound the same in your head.

One of our clients was already working with us on clearing away her own clutter. She is a modern-day Renaissance woman, deeply involved in a successful career. Her other passions included arts and crafts, gardening, and racing automobiles. Walking into her home, you were as likely to see a gear shift knob, gardening gloves, or a glue gun on the table.

We were making progress on organizing her home when Debra called one day to say, "My mother died last week. Can you meet me at her place and let me know what's involved in clearing out her house? My sister thinks we should put it up for sale before winter sets in."

The address she gave me led to one of the big rambling homes in the oldest part of town. After walking thorough the house, I realized that her mother had a unique way of dealing with clutter. Like many people, she made stacks of papers. What made her unique was that as the stacks of papers piled, up she would put them in a dresser drawer. When one dresser filled to overflowing, she would buy another dresser and fill that one up, too.

Living Clutter-Free Forever

There were more than fifty dressers in a house of eighteen rooms. It took three people eleven days to sort through everything from old Vogue and Butterick dress patterns, to recipes, to stock certificates, to church bulletins from 1962. In this whole process, I watched Debra agonize over decisions her mother had given up making years before. Now it fell to a bereaved daughter to make every one of those decisions.

Deb looked up at me in tears at one point and said, "I hope I don't do this to my family. I want so much to mourn my mother, and right now I'm resentful that she left so much confusion behind."

So how do you prevent your family from ever having to deal with the toughest clutter challenge of all? Ask yourself three questions:

1. If disaster were to strike today, who would get the job of clearing out all my stuff, and how would that job affect them?
2. What can I get rid of today that can spare my family pain or trouble in the future?
3. What can I give, donate, or assign to others that will leave behind a legacy I most want to be remembered for?

Question 2. WHAT'S ONE OF THE BASIC "TRUISMS" ABOUT ORGANIZING THAT IS JUST PLAIN WRONG?

We'd love to rewrite the old saying, "A place for everything and everything in its place." The saying is half right. You do need a place for everything. And the slogan would be fine if it stopped there. A place for everything, period.

The reality is that life is a contact sport. Every single day, you have contact with people and things. Stuff gets out of place and you only drive yourself and others crazy if you insist that everything stay in its place. So take stuff out, use it, enjoy it, work with it, and play with it. Engage life in all its abundant possibilities. And then put that stuff away. In its place.

Ah, but there's the problem. There's often no specific place to put an item. Sometimes you stick it in a drawer, sometimes on the refrigerator, sometimes under the counter, and sometimes in the supply cabinet. So in the meantime, you put it in a corner somewhere, thinking, "I'll put that away later."

Any item in your possession that doesn't have its own home creates automatic clutter.

Living Clutter-Free Forever

So every piece of mail, every remote control, every newspaper or magazine, every business card, every stalk of celery needs a home. From this moment forward, you can quit postponing the decision about where that home should be. Make yourself a front-door promise. Stand in front of a mirror. Raise your right hand. Look yourself in the eyes and say, "I promise I won't let anything into my home or office that I'm not willing to make a specific place for."

Are you already thinking of a loophole? Are you thinking you can sneak things in through the back door? Then remember what you've known all along. When you play games with yourself, you are always the winner. And you are always the loser, too.

Question 3. SOME OF MY CLUTTER IS HARDER TO DISLODGE. ARE THERE DIFFERENT TYPES?

Yes, there are four clutter categories:

SITUATIONAL

Situational clutter arises from specific events. You are engaged in a project that generates a temporary mess. This is a natural and normal part of life in a complex world.

To conquer situational clutter, recognize its temporary nature, set an end point by which it will all be cleaned up, and move on with your life.

EMBEDDED

Embedded clutter reflects years of accumulation and benign neglect. The longer you have lived or worked in a specific setting, the deeper the layers go. Many people report that an extended campaign to banish embedded clutter takes at least one month of focused clean-up activity for each year they have been in the setting. Naturally, if you are getting ready to move, you may have to do the job in a few weeks. So instead, you put everything in moving boxes and promise yourself you'll organize everything when you get settled. (And the clutter cycle begins again.)

To conquer embedded clutter, set starting and ending timeline goals, arrange incentives or support along the way, and plunge in.

IMPENDING

Impending clutter is everything around you that is sitting in a pile waiting for you to make a decision about where it needs to go. It's the stacks of mail, leftover project materials, stuff you heap on the bottom stair waiting for someone to take it up to the next floor. Again, these pre-clutter piles and stacks and clusters of stuff are a normal part of living. But they become fixtures if neglected for long. Clutter is contagious. But order and clutter discipline can also become contagious.

To conquer impending clutter, create and follow systems to clear all flat surfaces at least once a week—and be sure that everything has a place.

INVITATIONAL

Invitational clutter is the most invisible, and therefore the most problematic. This is clutter you generate unintentionally by operating in today's society. These are things you "invite" into your setting without considering whether they still have value for you. This may include any magazines you will never read, unwanted catalogs that seem to just keep coming, a surplus of small gifts people give you because they know you like roosters, or stuff-of-the-month items you "don't have time" to cancel.

To conquer invitational clutter, you must first recognize your role in creating this mess. Second, clarify what you do and don't want in your ideal setting and stop opening yourself to the invasion of anything that no longer matches your vision. Third, purge your current excess, cancel subscriptions, get off mailing lists, and announce your rooster collection complete.

Question 4. WHAT'S THE MOST UNUSUAL BENEFIT YOU'VE SEEN ANYONE GAIN FROM A CLUTTER CAMPAIGN?

We've had clients report a wide range of benefits – some of them unexpected. People have said it helped them:

- Locate long-lost items
- Enjoy their family and work more
- Reduce distractions
- Free square footage in their house (and even their heart and head!)
- Discover hidden treasures
- Get rid of guilt generators
- Renew their peace of mind
- Find more time for romance and play.

Here's a sample letter from someone with yet another unexpected benefit.

> *"Thank you for transforming my life. I had always considered myself hopelessly stuck in a clutter trap. I took courses on time management, read good books on organizing, even worked with a consultant for one session. I knew all the tips and techniques. Everything helped for a while, but the clutter always came back.*

"Then I learned your five steps. I decided to try them, thinking to myself, 'Here's another quick fix that can at least keep me sane through the holidays.' I was so wrong.

"I really got the message. Use a systematic process to focus on eliminating clutter come-back. That one shift gave me the energy to go through the whole process. It wasn't as fast as I'd hoped. It still isn't always easy. But it works.

"I got my room, my house, and my office in order. As I finally tackled the attic and garage, I noticed something amazing. I was also losing weight. The more stuff I got rid of, the more I could see how little it takes to make me happy. I guess I started to think of food that way too. (Is clutter a secret form of 'comfort food?')

"I'm not sure of the dynamics of all this. All I know is that I feel happier, healthier, more energetic and free, and even thinner!

"Since my setting now supports my daily needs and nourishes my dreams, I choose to keep it this way. For me personally, here's to clutter-free forever!"

LOVE IT OR LOSE IT

We can't promise you exactly the same benefits, but you will indeed be surprised at the difference your personal Clutter Campaign can make in your life.

Question 5. BUT MY REAL PROBLEM IS OTHER PEOPLE. HOW DO I CHANGE THEM?

"At work, people give me stuff I have to keep. I don't have a choice," one client complained. "And at home, other people's clutter drives me crazy."

The shortest path to frustration and failure is to try to change other people. Your most powerful path to sustained success is to start with yourself first and let those around you be affected by observing your increasing calm, focus and relaxed success.

Those of us in the "real world" fight this idea. We want some magic potion or power to get our kids to clean up their rooms, or colleagues to stop leaving old half-full coffee mugs around till they get moldy. That's what we want and we try every way we can think of to get those results. We threaten, we ask, we tease, we plead, we cajole, maybe we even bring in the big gun and try guilt. Nothing seems to work. They remain immune.

If all our tactics have failed in the past, perhaps it's time to try a new approach. Tell yourself a new story about the amazing level of power and control you have over one person in the universe — you. Say to yourself, "I am a single atom of order, balance, and harmony. I move through my world radiating relaxed resourcefulness. I create and sustain an environment that helps me love my life and work. I encounter challenges and move through or around them. I don't allow anything to rob me of my freedom to create the results I want in my life."

In other words, change what you can (you). Accept what you cannot change (everyone else), and waste no energy fighting the difference.

One woman had reached the absolute limit of endurance with her son's cluttered room. She tried everything she could think of to get him to keep it reasonable for habitation. She finally told him, "Tom, today I'm shutting the door on your room, and I won't open it again until you leave for college or career. As long as nothing crawls out, leaks out or smells, I will not go in there again."

For six years she did not go into his room. A few years later, when her son had moved into a place of his own, her daughter called to report, "Mom, I just went over to see Tom's new apartment. You wouldn't believe it. He's got it so orderly, clean, and organized. He even has one of those key holders by the back door. I thought I was visiting you."

When you, yourself, are the model for order, you never know who is watching and learning. So remind yourself about the power you have over your own decisions. Start there.

Question 6. HOW DO I SET UP A CLUTTER CAMPAIGN GROUP?

One client commented, "I'm ready to plunge in and get organized, and I know that if I try to do this alone, I'll lose my good intentions after a few weeks. What can I do to hold on to my focus and energy?"

If you are the kind of person who prefers an exercise class or a gym buddy to provide structure for your fitness resolution, there may be a helpful answer. Let the power of friends and colleagues, or the fear of reporting "no progress," help spur you on. Here are some ideas for creating a team for your Clutter Campaign. Note that this is not called, "The bunch of people who like to get together and talk and hang out, in hopes that our homes and offices will magically organize themselves." This is called a Clutter Campaign, because it works best when people invest commitment, passion, and energy — together.

- Assemble a group of 2-10 people committed to finding their clutter freedom. These people can be from your neighborhood, your gym, your church, your work, or your school.
- Create a structure that provides support, flexibility, and accountability.
- Work on the five steps or any of the thirty options, one at a time, making individual adaptations to match varying needs and styles.
- Meet regularly to share successes, snags and next steps. These sessions can be lunch-and-learn sessions at the office, over coffee at your local deli, in the spectator stands as your kids play soccer, or any location where it is convenient and comfortable to gather and talk.
- Help each other between sessions by serving as problem solvers or encouragers.
- Celebrate successes.

Your structure can range from a simple weekly coffee chat with a friend, to a structured group with an agenda for each session. Some people get creative and host special events. One group has an annual white-elephant party where each person brings sev-

LOVE IT OR LOSE IT

eral unwrapped items they don't want or need. They trade with others in the group and the host donates all the remainders to Goodwill Industries.

Another group encouraged each member to research one local charity they wanted to support. At each session of the group, one member describes the charity, describes the people they help, and the donations they need. Twice a year, members bring items that fit the need profile of those charities and the advocate collects them for delivery. So twice a year, these friends clear away clutter and contribute to their community at the same time. "I always wanted to be involved in community service," reports one group member. "But my work kept me too busy. Now I feel like I am contributing. It feels good. And it helps me stay aware of how much I have to be grateful for."

The variations are endless. But there are four things most of the successful Clutter Campaign groups have in common:

1. A structure that keeps the members focused on their goals.
2. They hold themselves accountable for the promises they make.
3. They support one another.
4. They celebrate their successes.

Question 7. DO I HAVE TO DO ALL FIVE OF THE STEPS?

Not necessarily. Only the ones where you want to succeed. That's a somewhat irreverent response to a question we hear often. But here's the truth. In more than 25 years of working with people from ambassadors to artists, from CEOs to moms-on-the-go, from corporate lawyers to community leaders, we have seen these steps work to help people create and sustain an environment they love. The steps support an active, fluid, dynamic life process that gets rid of clutter and keeps it from coming back.

Here's a glimpse at the specific snags you are likely to encounter if you take action on four of the steps, but leave one neglected.

If you don't DESIGN YOUR VISION, you can still produce good short-term results in getting an area clean and organized. But you feel no sense of completion or commitment to maintaining an environment you have never defined as your idea setting. You may hear yourself saying, "I'm not sure what I want, but I don't think I'm there yet."

If you don't ELIMINATE YOUR EXCUSES, you may feel partially successful, but something always erupts that allows you to shift blame or responsibility to the circumstances or people around you. You may hear yourself saying, "It's not my fault."

If you don't COMMIT YOUR TIME you stay in the ready, ready, ready, mode, but never know where to start, or get around to taking action. You continue to wallow in clutter. You may hear yourself saying, "I just don't have the time."

If your don't SELECT YOUR TOOLS you dutifully follow all the steps but hate the process. You just want to be left alone to go back to doing things your way. You know the improvements won't last. You may hear yourself saying, "I'll do it, but I hate it."

If you don't MAINTAIN YOUR SUCCESS you get your setting the way you want it, and expect it to stay that way — in spite of changing dreams or circumstances. You may hear yourself saying, "Why can't things just take care of themselves?"

So the steps work better when they work together.

Question 8. WHAT'S THE SINGLE, MOST LOGICAL TIME TO UNCLUTTER?

Most people are reluctantly pushed to unclutter when they are moving! Planning a move increases your clarity about which items you treasure, and which ones are just taking up space in your life. Sorting through your belongings for a move is like a time-compressed evaluation of everything you own. As one client said, "If I wouldn't want to pay to have this thing hauled 3,000 miles across country, why should I let it sit here today?"

The five steps can save you time and money during a move. One woman reported that she had started her moving process by working through Step One for the home she was leaving, and also for the one her family was moving to. "It was easy to design a vision for the home we were leaving. I just pictured that everything would be empty in three weeks. Then I focused in great detail on the primary areas of the new place, and donated, or got rid of everything that did not fit. This was a great contrast with my earlier move. In that move I ran out of time and moved everything, planning to sort it all out later. Months later, some boxes were still unpacked, and unwanted toys and furniture clogged half the garage."

One of our clients says that she goes through her files, her home, and her closets once a year, questioning whether she would keep each item for a long-distance move. "I try to do it near April 1. It's a blend of an April Fool's exercise for myself and a reminder of the spring cleaning we always did when I was a kid. I get rid of enough stuff that I usually sense an overflowing of the fresh, new feeling of spring."

Question 9 - WHAT'S THE ONE THING I COULD CHANGE IMMEDIATELY THAT WOULD MAKE THE BIGGEST DIFFERENCE?

The single thing you could do immediately is to hold the vision of what is possible. Think again about the influence your setting has on your thoughts, and on your actions as you go through the day. Think about your ability to operate at your highest level when you are surrounded by an ideal environment. Say the following words, slowly, out loud to yourself:

This setting
supports and nourishes
everything I am,
or wish to be,
everything I do,
or need to do,
and nothing extra weighs me down.

This place is:
my safe harbor,
my comfortable resting point,
my relaxing retreat,
my invigorating environment,
my powerful springboard,
my welcoming haven,
my simple serenity,
my effortless embrace.

I make a daily choice to
know what I want (my vision)
and move toward what I want
instead of focusing on
what I'm trying to escape.
I make a daily choice
to live clutter-free forever.

See if those words, or others like them, help you hold your vision when there's one more closet to clean, or one more holiday meal to recover from.

Several readers have taken the words, edited or expanded the list, and read them onto an audiotape for themselves. They play the tape regularly to remember what is possible, remember what is desirable, and stay inspired.

LOVE IT OR LOSE IT

One last thought. We live in times both perilous and promising. Your work and your family need you to be at your best. Anything that drains you, depletes you, even distracts you, is robbing you from operating at your best. Where you go now is up to you. You can do as much or as little as you like. Your return will be in proportion to your investment.

What we have seen is that this definable process works in thousands of settings. It can work for you too

ENLIST WIDE-RANGING RESOURCES TO BECOME CLUTTER-FREE

WWW.LoveItOrLoseIt.com is your continuing resource for updated enrichment for your journey toward clutter-free living. Whether you are working at your own computer or borrowing time at the local library, this site offers stories, strategies, and sources more current than any book can update. We will also feature invitations to unique on-line and audio learning events. So come visit us online and see what is new and available to you right now!

Index

LOVE IT OR LOSE IT

A NOTE FROM BARBARA HEMPHILL

I grew up in Nebraska where my family shared the second floor of a tenant farmhouse. Our house got messy, but we had to be able to clean it up in five minutes or less if the minister was coming by after church on Sunday.

Many years later, lessons and principles from that childhood helped shape the business I started in 1978 with a $7 ad in a New York City newspaper.

My business flourished. One of my greatest rewards over all these years has been hearing from clients who said their lives were transformed, their relationships were improved, their businesses prospered, and their spirits were renewed.

This book was born in response to other clients who still had some challenges. They usually said something like:

1. *I can clean up the clutter, but it seems to come right back.*
2. *My problem is much more than the paper and the files.*
3. *I need a comprehensive system that goes beyond tools and techniques.*

I worked with Maggie, a long-term friend and colleague, to create the book they were asking for. Here's hoping it helps you, too.

LOVE IT OR LOSE IT

BARBARA'S BACKGROUND

·Author of:
- · *Taming the Paper Tiger at Home*
- · *Taming the Paper Tiger at Work*
- · *Simplify Your Workday*

Content provider for the *Taming the Paper Tiger* ® software

Developer of the "Productivity Quickstart™" for organizations and the "24-Hour Miracle™" for individuals. Both programs organize offices "starting with the desktop."

Past president of the National Association of Professional Organizers

Appeared on NBC's Today Show, CBS This Morning, CNN, and Good Morning America

Speaks to thousands of people each year

Wife, mother, step-mother, business owner, community volunteer, author, speaker, consultant, Barbara is based in Raleigh, North Carolina.

A NOTE FROM MAGGIE BEDROSIAN

I'm a reforming classic clutterer. I grew up sharing a room with my younger sister, and I could always blame the mess on her. Then I finished school, moved away, started a business, started a family, and could always blame the mess on being "too busy."

Finally in 1996 I had a transforming moment. My office was selected to undergo a BEFORE and AFTER makeover, and be photographed for a national magazine. Between the two photo sessions, a professional organizer helped me get it all cleaned and organized. I was amazed at the liberating joy of a clutter-free environment.

I was equally amazed to find that this clutter-free area inspired me to bring order, harmony, and ease to other areas of my home. Just as the clutter had been contagious, now clutter-freedom was contagious!

I soon recognized how closely the process meshed with my studies on how people focus on clarity to create more balance in their lives. Barbara and I talked about these similarities at length, and decided to write this book.

We hope it helps you feel your own liberating joy, of living and working in a place you love.

LOVE IT OR LOSE IT

MAGGIE'S BACKGROUND:

Author of:
- *Life Is More Than Your To-Do List: Blending Success And Satisfaction*
- *Delights, Dilemmas, And Decisions: The Gift Of Living Lightly*
- *Speak Like A Pro: A Tool For Marketing And Managing*

Former host of television's *Spotlight on Business*

Past president, American Society for Training and Development, Washington DC Chapter

Past President, National Speakers Association, Washington DC Chapter

Co-Founder, Washington Writers Workshop

Presenter of student and staff programs at Johns Hopkins University, University of Maryland, Marymount University, Indiana State University, and Mindanao State University

Former Peace Corps Volunteer

Wife, stepmother, business owner, community volunteer, executive coach, speaker, Maggie is based in Rockville, MD.

11 PM Wednesday night...sitting in my NEW office...both sets of sliding doors wide open...68 degrees...breezes...mini-water-fountain flowing gently...soft instrumental music playing...family sleeping...now back online...feel pretty good.

My friend and I started our Clutter Campaigns together. She thrives on structure and followed all the steps in perfect order. I found inventive variations to keep me intrigued and interested. So, it worked for both of us. We had fun playing off our differences, while both getting great results.

For me, these ideas are like the "inner game of organizing." I already have four other good organizing books with helpful tips. This one inspired me, though, to finally use the information I already had.

Everyone in our office completed the LOVE IT OR LOSE IT Inventory, focusing on our work setting. We discussed our results, and explored how to make our workplace more functional. Within a week, we had cleared away a lot of clutter from our area. Work seems to flow more smoothly now and we find what we need much more easily.

My two favorite ideas are the "front door promise" and the "rainy day jar." They are both so simple and practical that I they made an immediate difference for me and my family. Thanks for keeping it real.

Hemphill Productivity Institute
Home of Kiplinger's *Taming the Paper Tiger*

Our Mission:
We help individuals, families and organizations
to create and sustain a productive environment
so they can accomplish their work
and enjoy their lives.

FREE ezine
www.ProductiveEnvironment.com

800-427-0237 (in the U.S.)
919-773-0722 Office
919-773-0383 Fax

Virtual Assistant, DJ Watson
850-484-4111
djw@ProductiveEnvironment.com

www.LoveItOrLoseIt.com

SHARING CLUTTER-FREE LIVING
WITH OTHERS...

To order additional copies of this book
(bulk discounts available), call
800-427-0237

Or visit **www.LoveItOrLoseIt.com**

To contact Barbara Hemphill or Maggie Bedrosian
about presenting a session
for your meeting or conference, call
800-427-0237

Or visit **www.ProductiveEnvironment.com**
for more information on
creating and sustaining
an environment
that helps you
enjoy your life and work.